ENGAGING ALL FAMILIES

CREATING A POSITIVE SCHOOL CULTURE BY PUTTING RESEARCH INTO PRACTICE

STEVEN M. CONSTANTINO

Rowman & Littlefield Education
A division of
ROWMAN & LITTLEFIELD PUBLISHERS, INC.
Lanham • New York • Toronto • Plymouth, UK

This title was originally published by ScarecrowEducation.
First Rowman & Littlefield Education edition 2009.

Published in the United States of America
by Rowman & Littlefield Education
A Division of Rowman & Littlefield Publishers, Inc.
A wholly owned subsidiary of The Rowman & Littlefield Publishing Group, Inc.
4501 Forbes Boulevard, Suite 200, Lanham, Maryland 20706
www.rowmaneducation.com

Estover Road
Plymouth PL6 7PY
United Kingdom

British Library Cataloguing in Publication Information Available

Library of Congress Cataloging-in-Publication Data

Constantino, Steven M., 1958–
  Engaging all families : creating a positive school culture by
putting research into practice / Steven M. Constantino.
      p. cm.
  Includes bibliographical references and index.
  ISBN-13: 978-1-57886-062-3 (alk. paper)
  ISBN-10: 1-57886-062-8 (alk. paper)
  1. Home and school—United States. 2. Education,
Secondary—Parent participation—United States.
  3. School environment—United States.
  4. Educational innovations—United States. I. Title.
LC225.3 .C65 2003
371.19'2—dc21   2003009342

∞™ The paper used in this publication meets the minimum requirements of
American National Standard for Information Sciences—Permanence of
Paper for Printed Library Materials, ANSI/NISO Z39.48-1992.
Manufactured in the United States of America.

This book is dedicated to the person who taught me the most about families: my son, Matthew.

CONTENTS

INTRODUCTION

Write about what you know.

—Mark Twain

How many times, upon learning that I am a high school principal, does someone say to me "I would *not* want your job"? I begin to wonder: Do *I* want this job? What am I doing in this job? How did I end up leading this school (or district)? Being a school leader is the most rewarding, challenging, frustrating, joyous, satisfying, delightful, intense, funny, scary, roller-coaster job anyone could ever have. It seems that right at the moment you consider your resignation (again), someone shares a piece of information with you about how your assistance or your belief in him or her was a school or career turning point. You get to hold the hand of a frightened kindergarten student and shake the hands of students at graduation. You have the unique ability to help people, whether it is one at a time, or hundreds at a time. Is it a difficult job? Absolutely! Those who choose to enter this arena are special, dedicated, hardworking individuals who sacrifice a great deal so that children can achieve at high levels in a safe and orderly environment. It is certainly not a job for everyone. It is for these special people—school leaders—that this book is written.

A school leader must have a vision for the school or district, and must be able to communicate that vision and convince stakeholders that the vision is worthy of their time, energy, and talent. But like so many other ideas in education, there seems to be great skepticism with regard to the importance of vision. If positive change is truly desired and the belief is held that all students can learn to their fullest capacity, then it is necessary to put into place those systems and processes that allow the space and flexibility for a vision to develop and for a school to implement the programs, practices, and policies that move the school toward that vision.

Mark Twain advised that we should write about what we know. Even though my experiences lie within the realm of high school, this book is designed for leaders of all types, as well as those who are working toward administrative certification. Most importantly, this book is a practitioner's guide . . . a recipe book, of sorts. Practitioners must seize the research available and bridge the gap between research, development, and practice.

OVERVIEW OF CHAPTERS

Chapter 1 defines family engagement and discusses a framework for the leadership necessary to not only engage families but to create positive school cultures. It sets the stage for turning research into practice, in part by introducing you to Stonewall Jackson High School. References to actual and tested programs and initiatives are found throughout the book. An interesting metaphor for the type of school reform proposed in this book can be found within the story of the main office counter, which is explored in chapter 1. To understand the importance of leadership, there must be a discussion regarding the vision necessary to lead public schools in the twenty-first century. The discussion of vision is limited to that of family engagement with schools.

Chapter 2 is a review of the pertinent research in family engagement and involvement and its enhancement of the academic achievement of all students. It also contains the author's research on the engagement practices of high school students and the resulting conceptual model. This research chapter provides a conceptual framework upon which the resulting assessment and practical engagement ideas for family engagement are presented in subsequent chapters.

Schools acting as community centers is a concept that is a central theme in the engagement of families in schools. It is necessary for school leaders to embrace the concept of community schools and to begin looking at those processes that can help to transform our schools into community schools. Chapter 3 is a discussion of the concept of community schools and discusses the federal 21st Century Community Learning Centers program and conceptual framework.

Technology plays an increasingly important and valuable role in shaping family engagement programs in schools across America. With the options available to school leaders, it seemed logical to share practical information and experience as to how leaders can identify the technology that will most benefit the engagement of all families. Chapter 4 is a discussion of available telecommunications and Internet technology, attributes of technology that directly benefit family engagement, and practical applications of that technology.

The evaluation of current practice is important for schools and school leaders to know so as to understand the strengths and weaknesses in efforts to promote family involvement and engagement. Chapter 5 presents the "Comprehensive Evaluation for Family Engagement" as well as information as to how this evaluation should be undertaken. School leaders can refer back to this chapter as they engage in the evaluation and determine their levels of family engagement policies, procedures, and practices.

The evaluation is divided into separate and distinct segments: (1) Does your school say welcome? (2) engaging all families, (3) community outreach, and (4) engaging families with students.

Chapters 6 through 10 are structured to respond to the questions presented in the comprehensive evaluation. School leaders are encouraged to complete the evaluation in the manner presented in chapter 5 and then consult the following chapters for ideas and tested practices in the processes necessary for engaging all families. Each of the chapters contains the exact questions found in the evaluation and provides detailed responses to each of the questions. School leaders who are looking to improve areas of weakness can find tested ideas and practices. All of the information presented represents practical applications of research-based information. Each of the practices and ideas is born directly from research strands. Hopefully, the ideas presented will act as catalysts for readers to expand those ideas and develop new ones.

Chapter 11 draws together the research and suggested practice to provide the impetus necessary for educators to make the commitment to creating family friendly schools. A brief discussion of outcomes based on research frames the discussion for the need to pursue family engagement practices in all schools. The relationships of family engagement and student engagement with their own learning, as well as student response to certain aspects of family engagement, are also mentioned in this concluding chapter. Appendixes referenced in individual chapters are found at the end of the book.

WHAT THIS BOOK IS AND IS NOT

Over the past eight years, I have been fortunate to work at a great school with great people and wonderful students. Through those years, the faces have changed but the commitment and desire to make our school the very best has glowed brilliantly within the hearts of the staff, students, and families. There was little belief that the school would finally be a success story in the eyes of the community it served. I was to be just another in a long line of principals who came and went. The staff had little hope that the new principal would last more than a year or two. But something different occurred—in many respects, something magical. The right people, ideas, commitment, vision, work ethic, and desire all converged on one school at one time and the results are simply astonishing. The focus on families and connecting them with the education of their children has made a huge impact on the success of our school and our ability to craft a positive school culture. Simply put: families make the difference.

I hope this book will inspire you to try new ideas and approaches, embrace change, understand that failure is inevitable and survivable, and that success is bountiful when one understands that in order to be successful, risks must be taken. To do this, I hope my experience as a principal will help establish some credibility with the reader.

While surfing Internet booksellers and searching the keywords *school reform*, about one hundred titles appeared. School reform is a great topic on which to write. If the author is somehow connected to education, then there are ideas about reform, or at the very least, opinions on those aspects of school reform that are the most important in helping students achieve. If the author is a critic of public education, then reform initiatives are used as punching bags, citing failure after failure, to which the answers commonly lie somewhere outside of the realm of public schools and neatly within certain political agendas.

Hopefully, this book is none of that. There are no opinions on classroom reform issues or the standards-based movement. The premise of this book rests with the idea that there are enough people trying to reform classrooms, assessment, curriculum, and even teaching itself. The platform upon which this book is built is this: The more educators engage families in the academic lives of their children, the more likely our students will perform at higher levels. Reforming what happens *outside* of classrooms is as important as the reform movement inside of classrooms. This is not to suggest that curriculum and instructional reforms, the need for more and improved professional development, and the need for assessment be cast aside or ignored. In addition to all of the necessary reforms within classrooms, so must there be attention paid to the world of our students and their families outside of classrooms and schools. Those arenas are impacting achievement much more than any of us realize. Before there can be achievement, there needs to be *engagement*.

PARENTS VERSUS FAMILIES

For many years, research regarding families and schools could be found under the general heading of *parent involvement*. Several years ago, researchers began to rethink the use of the word *parent*. As family structures become more diverse, continuing to use the word parent often left many families outside of the research. The fact of the matter is that the adults in many students' lives are not parents and the use of that term alienates a growing population of adults. Using the word *family* helps to include all of those adults who play a significant role in rearing children.

Involvement means different things to different people. With all of the definitions and attitudes about family involvement, it seems appropriate to adapt language that more concisely describes the purpose of the book. Through the review of recent research, the word *engagement* appears as a way to define family interaction with schools. Thus, the term *family engagement* is used throughout this book to represent the interaction between schools and families and the degree to which families are involved in the educational lives of their children.

THE IMPORTANCE OF FAMILIES

A great deal of the work done at Stonewall Jackson centers on engaging families and students in education. As a result, this book is devoted to creating positive school cultures by understanding the power of families and how to include them in the educational lives of their children. If educators embrace the concept of family engagement in school, true engagement, then we have taken a quantum leap toward helping all of our students learn at high levels by creating positive cultures within which all students can thrive. Personal research has proved to me that families are indeed an integral part of the reason students choose to be engaged or disengaged with their learning. But know up front, this book has one important and overriding premise: That *you* believe the concepts and that *you* are willing to stand up and tell whomever might be listening that *you* value the importance of these concepts. You cannot delegate vision.

Success can be distilled down to a few key words: values, beliefs, vision, relationships, culture, and hard work. The values we hold as educational leaders ultimately determine the kind of school we shape and lead. The beliefs we hold and the vision we have for students, families, and education can bring about important and new relationships between all constituencies, thus improving the culture of our schools. Lastly, and not surprisingly, success is not easy; it takes all of the properties mentioned above—with a good dose of hard work.

1

LEADERSHIP FOR FAMILY ENGAGEMENT

There is a familiar ritual that is repeated in homes all over America. At some point in a day, from dinner conversations to cell phone conversations to notes left on refrigerators, parents and families seek understanding and information about their children's daily school experiences. In the vast majority of cases, parents are ill equipped to ask the appropriate questions to garner responses that provide answers they seek. Usually, the question posed by most parents is "What did you do in school today?" Children of all ages answer this question with one word: "Nothing." If the parent is particularly curious or brave, there might be a follow-up question: "Do you have any homework?" To which most children reply "No." This ritual is often the sum total of educational conversation in homes between parents and their children. Parents and family members assume they have fulfilled their obligation to engage their children in a discussion about school, and children respond with answers they know will end the discussion.

Family engagement is not a new concept. For more than thirty-five years, research regarding family involvement in education has shown that children have advantages when their parents support and encourage school activities. School and family partnerships point to the family's role as the first and best educator of children and to the importance of family involvement in the educational lives of their children. These important partnerships link the involvement of families with schools as an indicator of student success.

Yet even though our system of education continues to acknowledge the important role of families in the academic success of children, little educational reform is focused on the development of programs, practices, procedures, and policies to encourage family engagement. Nor does it seem that a great deal of curriculum designed to prepare teachers and administrators focuses on this important topic. Of late, political perspectives of parental involvement have become an issue of school choice, rather than a collective and collaborative effort to engage families in the educational lives of children.

Steinberg (1996) poses very alarming findings as a result of ten years worth of studies by himself and several prominent social scientists. He concludes that an extremely high proportion of American high school students do not take school or their studies seriously. Further, he finds that the adolescent peer culture in contemporary America demeans academic success and that schools are fighting a losing battle against this peer influence. Lastly, he states clearly that American parents are just as disengaged from school as their children are. Considering the information and propaganda that floods our society, this problem of disengagement is not limited to high schools alone.

Let's return to our family desperately trying to garner information about their child's school day. When parents ask such ubiquitous questions as "What did you do in school today?" and "Do you have any homework?" they do so because they are not equipped to ask better questions or questions that center on more specificity with regard to a child's school day. Simply put, they get inadequate answers to their questions because their questions are inadequate. How, then, can parents ask better questions of their children? The answer lies in the degree to which parents and families are engaged with their children's academic lives and how schools and families work together to educate all children. Most importantly is the idea that schools become catalysts for seeking avenues to create partnerships with families so that information can flow from the school to home as well as from home to school.

In their book *Raising Self-Reliant Children in a Self-Indulgent World*, authors Glenn and Nelsen (1989) discuss the importance of true dialogue and state emphatically that without the ability for children to enter into dialogues with people who are important to them, it becomes difficult for children to see themselves as meaningful and significant. Families want to be engaged with their children's learning experiences in school. They want to know that their children are doing well and will succeed. All parents, regardless of their ethnicity or socioeconomic stature, want what is best for their children so that each child can prosper and exceed them in quality of life.

A DEFINITION OF FAMILY ENGAGEMENT

Joyce Epstein (1992) identified the six types of school-family-community involvement that include the basic obligations of families and schools as well as parental involvement at school and involvement in learning activities at home. The typology includes (1) home to school communication, (2) school to home communication, (3) parents as volunteers, (4) parent involvement in school governance and decision making, (5) positive home learning environment, and (6) greater collaboration and connection with the community. Epstein indicated that the sixth type of involvement was not part of the original research that helped identify the first five and admitted that this area opens a complex and unexplored arena and defines community as the child's home neighborhood and the wider local community of business, civic, cultural, religious, and other organizations and agencies that influence children's learning.

Patrikakou (1997) cites parental expectations of student achievement and Keith et al. (1998) adds parent–child communication as key factors in helping students succeed. Deslandes et al. (1996) as well as Hickman et al. (1995) both cite parent support as leading to better grades.

The actions of parents within the context of the educational lives of their children can be described in two categories, involvement and style. The involvement of parents or families includes the engagement of families in the instructional and noninstructional (cocurricular, extracurricular) lives of their children as well as the family's educational experiences and values about the importance of education. The style with which parents and families are involved in their children's school lives has more to do with the educational culture of the family rather than the socioeconomic level or other factors that are more widely perceived by educators. Schools that promote the true engagement of families not only help all students achieve but also can have an impact on the educational culture of families. Even though educators may not be able to affect a family's socioeconomic level, they very much can influence the educational culture of any family.

For purposes of this discussion, the definition of *family engagement* will be limited to those systems, processes, policies, procedures, and practices that allow parents and family to be a credible component within the academic lives of their children. Throughout this book, the words *parent* and *family* will be used interchangeably. Each defines those adults who play a significant role in caring for the child outside of the realm of school.

THE IDEA OF CULTURE

Defining the term *culture* can be somewhat daunting. Each author who writes about this subject has a unique perspective on the definition of the word. It certainly is not a term that we consciously think about each day as we prepare to work with our students, staff, and community, but many educators have come to believe in it more readily and understand that within the realm of developing positive school cultures lies the treasure of academic achievement for all students.

There exists excellent literature that focuses on professional learning communities and how leaders can improve their schools. A component of all of these ideas is the notion of school culture. It appears across a myriad of writing on the subject of improving schools. With an increasing emphasis on the notion of culture, it serves educators well to understand and define the term so as to begin the task of creating positive cultures in all schools.

One of the better descriptions of school culture emanates from the Southwestern Educational Development Laboratory (SEDL).[1] In their work on culture, they define it as the encompassing attitudes and beliefs of those inside the school environment and outside the school, or the external environment. Also included are the cultural norms of the school and the relationships between persons in the school. Attitude and belief are core issues

---

[1] For more information on SEDL, visit their website, www.sedl.org. This particular information comes from www.sedl.org/change/school/culture.html.

in the success of any school. In many respects, relationships contain actions and interactions of people. These relationships are built on attitudes and beliefs, which can also be defined as values. Think about your students for a moment. Do their attitudes about school and their teachers affect the degree to which they are successful? What about your staff: Do their attitudes and beliefs affect the outcomes of students? Do the attitudes of parents and families affect the operation of the school, the attitude and action of teachers, and the success of students? Do the interactions of all of these constituents positively support the mission of your school? It stands to reason that we must create positive school cultures in which students can thrive if we want them to have better academic success in school. A positive school culture cannot be developed if the vision of the school does not include engaged families.

THE IMPORTANCE OF SCHOOL CULTURE

School culture is of vital importance and is often overlooked as education becomes more standards driven. The study and implementation of positive school culture is important. John Goodlad (1984) reminds us that "alike as schools may be in many ways, each school has an ambience (or culture) of its own and, further, its ambience may suggest to the careful observer useful approaches to making it a better school" (81). When schools seek to improve, a focus on the values, beliefs, and norms of both the school and environment outside the school is necessary.

There is a general knowledge base regarding school culture. Patterson, Purkey, and Parker (1986) suggest the following attributes:

- School culture affects the behavior and achievement of elementary and secondary school students.
- School culture does not fall from the sky; it is created and thus can be manipulated by people within the school.
- School cultures are unique; whatever their commonalities, no two schools will be exactly alike—nor should they be.
- To the extent that it provides a focus and clear purpose for the school, culture becomes the cohesion that bonds the school together as it goes about its mission.

- Though we concentrate on its beneficial nature, culture can be counter-productive and an obstacle to educational success; culture can also be oppressive and discriminatory for various subgroups within the school.
- Lasting fundamental change (e.g., changes in teaching practices or the decision-making structure) requires understanding and, often, altering the school's culture; cultural change is a slow process.

The strength in understanding and supporting the notion of positive school cultures centers on the inclusion of those persons in the environment *outside* of the school, primarily families. Families are an integral part of cultural change in schools. Reform ideas presented in research and literature discuss important aspects of school reform; however, the idea of families being a component of each of the aspects is often lost. A certain level of naiveté exists in those who propose any type of school reform and do not include a component for families.

As important as the inclusion and engagement of families is the engagement of students and their peers within the environment of the school. A student-centered environment is an integral ingredient in a positive school culture. The larger the school, the more likely the leadership cannot devote energy to school culture and a student-centered environment. Engaging students in their own learning is tantamount to successful school achievement. In order to do this, though, families must be connected to the process.

AN ALTERNATIVE TO TESTING

Most school leaders face barrier and end-of-course testing mandates from our individual states. Now, with the recently enacted No Child Left Behind federal legislation, we may very well see more tests given to students to measure their mastery and outcomes. There are numerous stories of testing programs and the problems that need to be overcome so that schools can maintain accreditation and so that administrators and teachers can hang onto their jobs. The future of public education hangs gingerly in the balance, with the recent Supreme Court ruling upholding vouchers.

In his book *Reading, Writing, and Justice: School Reform as if Democracy Matters*, James Fraser provides an interesting perspective regarding standards in schools.

In fact, the split in the standards movement is very deep. On the one hand are those who argue that schools must be held accountable for high standards and for the success of every child in meeting the standards. On the other hand, there is a very different standards movement which argues that every child (and by extension their parents) must be held accountable for meeting the standards and if they don't it is their own fault and their own responsibility to correct the situation. . . . The latter approach demands relatively little in the way of investment. Set the standards. Offer the tests to see if the students meet them. Separate the winners from the losers. It is a fairly simple and inexpensive process. Of course, another question needs to be asked about the latter approach: "Has anything actually been done to raise standards by this move?" As the old Highland Scots saying goes, "You don't fatten a sheep by weighing it."

Educators are responsible for the learning of every child. The inherent challenges in this goal cannot and will not be met if we continue to ignore the concept of family engagement and its relationship to the academic achievement of all students within a positive school culture.

A VISION THAT INCLUDES FAMILIES

Vision is an essential component of creating a positive school culture. *Where there is no vision, the people perish.* Leaders must possess a vision in order to provide forward momentum to their organization. In tandem with possessing a vision is the notion that leaders must communicate that vision and convince stakeholders that the vision is worthy of their time, energy, and talent. But like so many other ideas in education, there seems to be great skepticism with regard to the importance of vision. Principals find themselves caught in the day-to-day quagmire and cannot even return phone calls let alone ponder their vision for the school.

School leaders who want positive change and believe that all students can learn to their fullest capacity need to put into place those systems and processes that will allow the space and flexibility to develop a vision for their school. In addition, they must implement the programs, practices, procedures, and policies to move the school toward that vision. Investing in this concept is necessary to achieve the desired outcomes.

An important component to vision is belief. Every school leader must believe that all students can learn at high levels. Every school leader must set high expectations for students and staff. Every school leader must believe that forging a positive, healthy, and meaningful relationship with families will bring about expectations and learning that benefit each and every student. It is this last belief that is most critical in establishing long-term success with family engagement. More often than not, school leaders profess to welcome the engagement of parents and families but take action, sometimes unconsciously, to limit or control such relationships.

RESEARCH INTO PRACTICE

At the juncture where research literature regarding family engagement, personal research and experience, knowledge of school administration, and the desire for reform to improve student achievement intersect begins the story of Stonewall Jackson High School and the commitment to involving all families in the educational lives of their children.

Stonewall Jackson High School is located in Manassas, Virginia, approximately thirty-five miles southwest of Washington, D.C. Stonewall Jackson is one of eight high schools within the Prince William County School Division. The school division serves approximately 60,000 students in seventy-six schools. Stonewall Jackson has a student population of 2,600 students in grades 9 through 12 on a seventy-acre campus. The school is diverse both socioeconomically and culturally. Stonewall Jackson draws its students from a full continuum of economic backgrounds: from subsidized and low-income housing, apartments, and government-subsidized housing projects, through lower-middle and middle-class suburban neighborhoods, to single-family estates worth more than a million dollars. A large percentage of the family population commutes eastward toward or into downtown Washington, D.C., in government, government-related, and military workplaces. Lower-income families tend to work in service-related jobs within and around the Prince William County area. From local bus drivers to corporate CEOs, there is a rich and interesting mix of economically diverse family structures. Free and/or reduced lunch statistics reveal that 21 percent of the student population have identified themselves as eligible for this program.

For the tenth time in a twenty-three-year period, the position of principal at Stonewall Jackson High School was vacant in early 1995. On the day that the board of education was to vote on the appointment of the tenth principal, the superintendent of schools and a board of education member invited the candidate to lunch. This meeting was an opportunity for the board member to have a personal and direct conversation with the selected candidate about the impending appointment prior to casting a vote that evening. Almost immediately, the conversation turned to the vast number of problems affecting the school that the candidate wished to lead.

Of the nine principals to have held the job, their tenures ranged from the longest record of five years to the shortest tenure of two days. The board of education member discussed significant staff morale problems, community perception problems, student discipline problems, as well as data that clearly showed a school in crisis. The candidate sat quiet, almost motionless; stunned by the information he was hearing and pondering his decision to accept this task. Even though there had been some rumors of problems at the school, the candidate never imagined the degree to which the school was in academic and social turmoil. Suddenly the board member posed a question to the candidate: What was it that the candidate was going to do as principal that had not already been tried by the previous nine? Close to being rendered speechless, the search for an appropriate answer was awkward. The answer centered on the need to assess the degree to which students and community were disengaged from the school and, working in tandem with all stakeholders, reengage—and perhaps even reinvent—a school. With that answer, the board member cast a leery look toward the candidate, wished him well, and announced that he was the last hope for a school that could suffer no more setbacks. The candidate was approved to be the tenth principal of Stonewall Jackson High School and began in the position on Monday, March 13, 1995.

During the period from 1995 to the present, several reform initiatives were developed and implemented to improve the achievement of students as well as improving the perception of the school with students, parents, and community. While reforms in curriculum, instruction, the instructional day, and programs all have made contributions to the improvement process, the programs established to promote family engagement and a student-centered culture within the school have been the focus of the present administration and the most recognized of the reform efforts. These efforts began in a very unusual and somewhat unorthodox manner upon the arrival of the new principal.

THE MAIN OFFICE COUNTER

Intimidated by the job he had accepted and exhilarated at the opportunity to make a positive difference, the new principal arrived early on his first day of work. Upon entering the main office via a large set of glass double doors, he met his first challenge. Affixed to the office wall was a large poster that read "Build it and they will come." He remembered thinking to himself, "Aren't *they* already here? What has not been built yet?" He then noticed the worn carpet, mismatched plastic chairs lined up against the wall, the clocks that did not tell the correct time, the years of neglect, the mismatched filing cabinets, the old wooden student desks used to prop up typewriters, and *the counter*.

The counter was about fifteen feet long. The walnut laminate had been picked away around the edges from students waiting to be assigned detention or had been broken by custodians as they vacuumed or cleaned. There it stood, a man-made barrier between the school and anyone who entered it. Behind the counter were the tops of two heads, presumably secretaries assigned to that office. It seemed like minutes, but probably wasn't, when he cleared his throat to see if he could get the attention of one of the two ladies. No luck. Finally, somewhat in despair, he said "Good morning." That seemed to work, as the secretary closest to him looked up and said, "Yes?"

"I'm the new principal."

"Oh, your office is over there," and she pointed toward her right and his left. With that she went back to her work. He later learned that it was her job to greet people. The secretary who continued to ignore the entire scene was not responsible for greeting people.

Did he think about the word *culture* when he walked in that morning? No. His instincts told him, however, that drastic change had to occur and had to occur relatively fast. Is that how everyone was treated when they walked in? The impression of the school culture, that being the backbone and lifeblood of the essence of the organization and what the organization stood for, was negative. *Welcome to our broken-down school where we hope we will make you feel as if you are imposing on us. Please take a seat in the mismatched uncomfortable plastic chairs while we decide if we are going to help you or not.*

The new principal began to think about the conversation with the board member. The lack of academic focus, the polarization of the faculty, lack of community involvement or support, student unrest, and on and on. It seemed to all be symbolized by his first impression of the main office and *the counter*. All of those problems were inherent in how the school presented itself, and how its employees presented themselves.

With those rather unflattering images, he set out to get rid of the counter, and before long it was gone. All that was left was a faint impression in the deteriorating carpet and the two secretaries who looked as if they had had all of their clothes suddenly ripped from their bodies. The story of the counter not only begins the reflection process with regard to the physical messages in a school building but the communication of ideals, culture, mission, and vision as well. In some respects, the counter represented everything that was wrong with Stonewall Jackson High School.

It is indeed a bit odd to center school reform around the removal of a main office counter, but the counter and its removal are symbolic. If one looks hard enough around a school, similar symbols can be found. Some are positive and some are negative. Perhaps it is the condition of the parking lot, sidewalks, or landscaping, or as simple as the cleanliness of the main doors. Whether a school is suburban, urban, or rural, the messages sent both physically and subliminally have a tremendous impact upon all who enter a school.

THE NEED FOR LEADERSHIP IN FAMILY ENGAGEMENT

Leadership is walking the walk, engaging and believing in people, selling ideas and concepts, listening to customers, and creating a school where students achieve and where families are an integral part of the process. A school where teachers have significant training and where standards are high. A school where everyone, including the principal, models excellence. A school where there are no bad ideas and where everyone, including students and their families, is encouraged to take risks. A school where leadership is truly shared and collaboration is a real process, not a neat paragraph in the school plan gathering dust in a drawer. Good leadership starts with a vision of what can be.

Schools should broaden their efforts to welcome and invite families into the school setting. Although families all over the country are seemingly involved with their children and have generally positive feelings about the school, the degree to which they are physically present in the school, whether it be the normal school day or after school for activities and events, is minimal. With the exception of back-to-school nights, families are generally not physically present in the school building, even though students report that their parents feel welcome. Events involving the entire community, including teachers, could be a powerful force in building the relationships necessary for schools to garner the partnerships they seek.

The style of parenting displayed by families can be enhanced and improved with efforts from the school. Schools can enhance the flow of positive communication between families and students by providing to them information about classes, assignments, grades, activities, and other school-related topics. Most families can and will discuss these topics with their children, and children generally appreciate knowing that their parents care enough to discuss issues, concerns, ideas, and school happenings. Because of the interaction of students, their friends, and their friends' families, information provided by the school might not only be communicated between parent and child but will very likely be communicated between children and their friends' parents, thus building a strong foundation for a positive school culture. School leaders must focus not only the reforms necessary within classrooms but also those that contribute to positive school cultures and engaged communities. Outside influences, like friends, families, jobs, and church, all have an impact on student performance.

A vision for developing a positive school culture must begin with the leadership of schools and districts. Believing that true family engagement can assist in helping all students achieve is a notion that cannot be delegated to a subordinate's "to do" list or begin and end as a neatly worded postscript in a school district's strategic plan. Engaging families with schools is a process; the catalyst for that process is the leader.

2

WHY FAMILY ENGAGEMENT?

A large body of research supports the simple notion that students achieve more when their families are engaged with school. Hundreds of books and articles have been written on this subject. The purpose of this book is not to restate what has already been diligently documented, but rather to give school leaders practical and tested ideas so that they might pursue positive school cultures through family engagement.

With this said, however, a salient point must be addressed. The ubiquitous nature of family engagement research should not be a reason to ignore emerging ideas in the field. The quality of the processes and systems within our schools relies heavily on our ability as leaders to use research and data to understand the very nature of our schools and to assist us in shaping a vision of what could be. This chapter is designed to give an overview of foundational theories and current thinking within the realm of family involvement.

UNDERSTANDING THE NEED FOR FAMILY INVOLVEMENT

The evolutionary nature of the relationship between public schools and their students suggests a need for continued activity in the area of school–family partnerships. In 1999, the percentage of homes operating below the poverty level was 11.9 percent for families from all races, 7.7 percent for whites, 23.6 percent for blacks, and 26.5 percent for Hispanics (U.S. Census Bureau 2001). Because of this poverty, many low-income families experience a kind of social stress, causing them to have difficulty promoting the social and psychological development that their children need to function successfully in school (Comer 1980). The country is also rapidly becoming more culturally diverse, with a decline in the white non-Hispanic population from 75.6 percent to 71.9 percent during the period 1990 to 2000, an increase in the black population from 12.3 percent to 12.9 percent, and increase in the Hispanic population from 9.0 percent to 12.6 percent during the same period (U.S. Census Bureau 2001).

THE IMPORTANCE OF A FAMILY-SCHOOL RELATIONSHIP

Barriers of time, cultural difference, socioeconomic status, and changing family structures impede partnerships between schools and families. The national PTA standards for parent and family involvement include an emphasis on regular, two-way, and meaningful communication between home and school; promoting and supporting parenting skills; and parents playing an integral role in assisting student learning (White 1998). Dodd (1998) echoes much of the same sentiment, placing a high value on schools providing parents with information in multiple ways and developing ways to involve parents as partners in learning.

There are other important benefits of family participation in the schools. Rich (1985) and Sattes (1985) found that parent involvement in education helped produce increases in student attendance, decreases in the drop-out rate, positive parent–child communication, improvement of student attitudes and behavior, and more parent–community support for the schools. Collaboration between home and school can also broaden both parents' and educators' perspectives and can help provide additional revenues, such as available Title I funding (Swap 1987).

The organization of society in previous decades caused a decline in parent involvement, forcing educators to work harder to garner family participation in education (Coleman 1991). Although researchers, educators, and families agree that improved family involvement is key to repairing many educational problems, few schools and communities have been able to achieve a sufficient involvement to produce a desired level (McLaughlin and Shields 1987). A genuine partnership between school and home is possible only when both partners have rich and frequent communication and when all parties are committed to forming lasting and effective partnerships (Bauch 1997). That partnership must include students as well.

Home has a significant influence on student achievement at school. For example, parent involvement can have a positive effect on the grades of high school students (Fehrmann, Keith, and Reimers 1987). When parents hold high expectations for their children, achievement in school is increased. Parent expectations and parent satisfaction are primary contributions to their child's success in school (Reynolds, Mavrogenes, Hagemann, and Bezruczko 1993). The home learning environment has a positive effect on a student's achievement in school and can have an effect on achievement that is three times as large as family socioeconomic status (Walberg 1984). This positive home learning environment includes informed parent–child conversations, encouragement of reading, and a focus on long-range goals. Students whose parents are aware of what their children are studying in school, who are in regular communication with their teachers, and who help to reinforce schoolwork show higher achievement all the way through secondary school (Ziegler 1987). It seems, then, that schools that are most successful in engaging parents and other family members in support of their children's learning look beyond traditional definitions of parent involvement.

BARRIERS TO SECONDARY
SCHOOL FAMILY PARTNERSHIPS

Family involvement in secondary school achievement is an important variable in student success. In a discussion and review of the benefits that secondary school students receive from strong family involvement, Connors and Epstein (1994) synthesize the research and conclude that activities such as holding high expectations for students, homework assistance, and sincere adult guidance in balancing and monitoring activities lead to higher achieving high school students.

As children get older and enter secondary school, there is a steep dropoff in the involvement of their families in education (Steinberg 1996). In one national study, for example, the percentage of parents of elementary school students who were involved in their children's education was 50 percent higher than among parents of secondary school students.

There are numerous efforts to explain this family involvement phenomenon. Hoover-Dempsey and Sandler (1997) indicate that the rigor and level of academic work required at the high school level changes parents' beliefs as to their ability to help their children and the emergence of adolescence suppresses an active interest in overt parental involvement. Secondary schools also tend to be more compartmentalized and no single teacher is primarily responsible for a particular student. Larger attendance areas create transportation and proximity problems that also discourage family involvement. Hollifield (1994) identifies the complex organization of the high school, the larger numbers of students assigned to individual high school teachers, and the physical numbers of students and families as deterrents to secondary school family involvement. Yet another idea touted by Steinberg (1996) indicates that secondary school parents transfer the complete responsibility for managing their children's education to the schools.

Secondary schools themselves must also accept responsibility for poor family involvement. Steinberg (1996) indicates that schools profess to understand and support family partnerships but their actual behaviors reflect mixed feelings as to the quantity and quality of family involvement. Often, while complaining about a lack of involvement from families, secondary schools set narrow parameters for controlled family participation.

Connors and Epstein (1994) indicate that family partnership programs in secondary schools should reflect the unique needs of the adolescent, such as the need for greater autonomy and responsibility, and the development of individual skills and talents. Further, the unique needs of families (such as working parents, proximity to the school, and a need to learn about the more complex secondary school organization) and the unique needs of secondary school teachers (such as having greater numbers of students and more families to involve) must also be considered.

The primary goal for family partnerships should center on students (Epstein 1992). To increase the motivation, achievement, and success of middle and high school students, secondary schools should have the needs, desires, attitudes, and opinions of students, as well as opportunities for students to demonstrate autonomy, accountability, and responsibility, at the core of any family partnership program. Partnerships built around students or for students may fail due to the lack of student participation in the process. Educators and parents cannot continue to teach students who may or may not wish to learn, but rather must partner with them and teach them to be lifelong learners. Families can assist with homework only when students understand that completing homework is essential for success. Families can attend school functions only when students are participating in school activities. Families cannot be involved if teachers do not see family involvement as their responsibility. In Connors and Epstein's (1994) survey, they found that while 90 percent of teachers felt family involvement in education was necessary, only 32 percent of teachers felt it was their responsibility to involve families. No students were surveyed regarding their attitudes, opinions, or suggestions for stronger partnerships. Topics that parents and students identify should drive family partnerships in all schools.

EPSTEIN'S MODEL OF OVERLAPPING SPHERES OF INFLUENCE

Epstein, director of the Center on Families, Communities, Schools, and Children's Learning, and often cited as one of our nation's leading researchers in the field of school, family, and community partnerships, developed a model of overlapping spheres of influence for school-family-community partnerships (Epstein 2001). Influencing the work of Epstein was Gordon (1979) who studied Head Start and Follow-Through programs and found that while positive effects of the programs on parents and young children were obvious, the relationship between involvement and influence was incomplete and that specific connections between parents and teachers were not measured.

Epstein (1995) emphasized the importance of this integration of school and family, and suggested that relationships of partnership between families and schools enhanced student achievement and encouraged families' participation in their children's education. According to Epstein, the three spheres of influence in the child's life—the school, family, and community—should overlap, putting the child at the center of the relationship. Epstein suggested that when the spheres of school, families, and community overlapped and engaged in true relationships of partnership, "learning communities or caring communities" (1995, 702) were born.

Epstein believed that separate contributions assume that schools and families are most efficient and effective when they each pursue independent goals and standards. An example of this is the practice of teachers to contact parents only when there is a severe problem or when it is too late for parents to intervene to solve a problem. Parents' and teachers' contributions to child development and education assume that early years determine later successes and parents have responsibility for first critical stages. Later, young adults assume the major responsibility for their own education. When schools and families work together in a collaborative partnership, students begin to receive the message that school is important, thus legitimizing their own work. According to Epstein, schools that are comprehensive in nature and that subscribe to the typology within her model help parents create home environments for learning, involve them in the decision-making structure of the school, communicate more effectively with the schools, and help parents to become productive volunteers and to take responsibility for supporting and motivating their children. With a focus on the sixth and newest type of family involvement (the connection and collaboration with the greater community), it stands to reason that broader investigations into "a child's home neighborhood" and other organizations that influence students' learning should include a discussion of peers as a component of the community sphere.

CURRENT RESEARCH IN FAMILY ENGAGEMENT

The most current research continues to describe the variances that exist in the ways schools and families work together. More often than not, these variances morph into general terms such as "parent involvement" or "school and community partnerships." School leaders should be interested in activities that engage parents and families both in the home and at our schools and realize the degree to which we can influence families with regard to their desires and dreams for their children. Given this rather wide and eclectic pool of research, finding a way to present it in a manner that is palatable and, more importantly, helpful to school leaders could fill this book. Short of that, it seems logical to focus on how families tend to be involved with schools and their children's education and review again the benefits to school leaders in acting as a catalyst in these important relationships.

School–family partnerships are now viewed as one of the components of school organization that may help to promote student learning and success in school. Having synthesized sixty-six studies and reports on family involvement, Henderson and Berla (1995) reported that studies have documented the following benefits for students: higher grades and test scores, better attendance and homework completion, fewer placements in special education, more positive attitudes and behavior, higher graduation rates, and greater enrollment in postsecondary education. Henderson and Mapp (2002) synthesized fifty-one additional studies and found that regardless of the income or background, students whose families were engaged with school were more likely to earn higher grades and enroll in higher-level programs, stay in school, and enroll in postsecondary education. This research summary also found that school initiatives to create programs and special efforts to involve and engage families did make a difference in student academic performance. Families, teachers, and schools can benefit from school and family partnerships. These important relationships lead to improving parental knowledge of their children's development, their ability to parent, their ability to assist their children with school and learning, and the quality of relationships between all stakeholders (Epstein 1992).

Generally speaking, families are engaged in learning through homework that has been designed to promote collaboration between the parent and child. Schools that develop training programs for parents to help them learn about specific subjects and school materials also go a long way to promote partnerships and student achievement (Clark 1993; Cooper, Lindsay, and Nye 2000). This effort to promote positive communication about school-related issues also advances the efforts to create home learning environments that are conducive to the achievement of all students. The more parents can help children outside of school, the better the child's chances of success in school (Shumow 2001).

Communication between families and schools, as well as interactions between families and school personnel, center on the relationship between teachers and parents. Also of significance is the ability for schools to share with families information about school events and school policies (Chrispeels and Rivero 2000). Generally speaking, parent participation in school organizations seems to be concentrated within the realm of parent–teacher organizations, school governance councils, and volunteering (Mapp 1999).

Catsambis (1998) and Yonezawa (2000) found that interactions about school-related issues between parents and children often centered on advice and guidance regarding school and academic issues as well as placement in specific courses. There is also evidence that parents can enhance their children's education by connecting community and nonschool activities to their children's in-school experiences (Cairney 2000; Gutman and McLoyd 2000; Tapia 2000).

Lastly, parents and families are already involved in school reform efforts, including advocating a need for school change, the development of standards-based educational programs within specific schools and districts, and participating with the development of improvement plans through local school governance councils (Desimone, Finn-Stevenson, and Henrich 2000; Dodd and Konzal 1999).

It is the school that dictates the type of relationship, partnership, or engagement program for families. Honig, Kahne, and McLaughlin (2001) contend that schools have adopted family involvement programs to try to "fix" students, giving classroom teachers more opportunity to teach successfully. This process seems to be in place of what should be happening—a general reshaping and rethinking of an individual student's school experiences in his or her own education and an understanding of what is impacting the student inside and outside of school. Many family involvement programs create teaching assistants out of parents rather than capitalizing on the teacher as the first and best educator of a child (Edwards and Warin 1999). Researchers agree that definitions of family involvement that are dictated by the school may fall short of the palate of options that can be in place to enhance much more than school goals, and include family goals as well.

THE RELATIONSHIPS NECESSARY FOR ENGAGEMENT

Additional research suggests that a significant proportion of students are disengaged from their learning and that peer culture demeans academic success. Parents are just as disengaged from school as their children (Steinberg

1996). A case study analysis of high school students at a large, comprehensive high school was undertaken to investigate the interaction of family involvement and peer relationships on the engagement practices of students. The effects of families and peers, as well as school influences and the individual student themselves, resulted in five forces for engagement: desires, attitudes, motivation, behaviors, and actions. Figure 2.1 represents the model that resulted from this research (Constantino 2002).

THE FOUR SPHERES OF INFLUENCE

There are numerous points where peers, individual students, schools, and families overlap their influence, which ultimately results in a continuum of student engagement from minimal engagement to significant engagement. What emerged from this study was a phenomenon that occurs as a result of the interaction of families, peers, individual students, and schools. Data that emerged from the study clearly show that student engagement in school is predicated on five forces for engagement: desires, attitudes, motivation, behaviors, and actions. Schools can promote the engagement of students by encouraging the involvement of families in the educational lives of high school students and by supporting program offerings of both instructional and noninstructional natures. Families of students have influence on their children's relationships with peers and there is significant interaction between students and the families of their peers. For purposes of this discussion, summaries of the school and family sphere follow.

School

Most significant in the data collection and analysis is the emergence of the school as a sphere of influence rather than a component of the macrosystem of outside or other influences that surround the overlapping spheres. It became clear that the school plays a more central and prominent role in shaping engagement practices of students.

Students interviewed for this study see the role of teachers as a critical aspect of the school's influence upon them. The school environment and its efforts to promote a positive culture are noticed and appreciated, but teachers are clearly

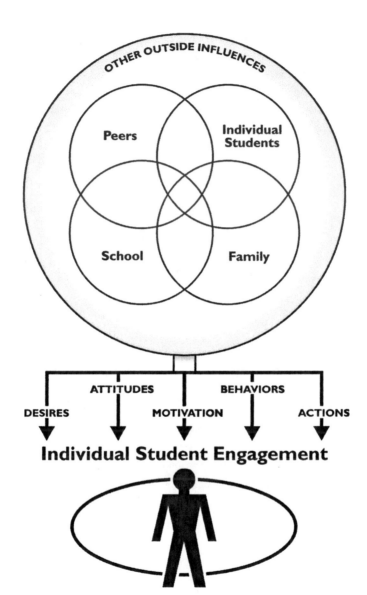

Figure 2.1. The Model for Student Engagement

a driving force within the school sphere with respect to the individual engagement of students.

Teachers who recognize students for their efforts and assist them with their work, decisions, and socialization in school motivate them. Teachers who are seen as friendly and caring play an important role in determining the degree to which a student will provide the necessary effort to be engaged and successful in a class. Students quickly understand teachers who may not be engaged with their own teaching and thus provide no encouragement for engagement in learning. However, even in those cases where a teacher may not be providing the necessary motivation, it is the notion of the importance of school that seems to provide the motivation to engage and be successful among some students and overrides negative teacher, family, or peer forces.

The school's efforts to promote positive peer relationships and provide avenues for students to participate and garner a sense of belonging do not go unnoticed. Students report a high level of interaction with programs designed to help them acclimate into the school culture and fulfill a basic sense of belonging. Coupled with this are efforts to provide an inviting and inspiring environment within which students can take ownership and pride. Generally speaking, students reacted favorably to these school practices and, in some cases, found them to be a strong motivational force in their quest for success.

Family

The involvement of families in the lives of their children remains a strong component to student engagement in school and school-related activities within the sample of students interviewed. Families who are involved and engaged with their children and their children's schools can provide their children motivation to do well and achieve to their highest levels. Family expectations alone can be a driving force in student engagement.

It was obvious in the case study that the vast majority of students had strong feelings about their family and their family's involvement with school. For example, even though students were not overly enthusiastic about their parents' ability to access grade and attendance information with technology, they welcomed their parents' review either to celebrate their successes or to openly discuss problems in school. This interaction between students and their families seemed to be important in determining the engagement level of students. If parents used the information to praise their child or help their child, the interaction was welcome. However, if the information was used to belittle their child, demean their child, or punish their child, the information then became a deterrent to school engagement. Whether viewing this phenomenon positively or negatively, one cannot discount the important relationship between children and their families.

Families who maintained a positive attitude about their children's school helped their children be more engaged and successful. In some cases, students reported that there was a time when their families argued with school personnel and that terse relationships resulted in the students' withdrawal from school and specific classes. Students in the study were cognizant of the school's efforts to promote family involvement; in those cases where students reported no real encouragement for engagement from the school, they did report that the positive relationship between the school and their family helped promote more positive parent–child communication.

Students found that their parents' encouragement and goals for the future assisted them in focusing on their own school engagement. Parents who shared their dreams, goals, and desires with their children and continuously reaffirmed the importance of education were a prime force in the engagement of many students. Parents who chose to compare their children to other children or who fixated on certain aspects of school provided a clear deterrent to their child's engagement with school.

CONCLUSION

In order to be most productive and beneficial with efforts toward the engagement of families, it is necessary to rethink some emerging theory and a great deal of practice. Most importantly, understanding how children learn and realizing that there are numerous people in the life of a child who can either enhance or detract from that learning are essential for the long-term success of every child who enters our schools. The involvement of families in the educational lives of children is not in and of itself a cure-all for the woes of educating all children; however, a commitment to reciprocal connections between families and schools is a powerful beginning in shaping an environment in and around schools, which enhances the opportunities, engagement, achievement, and ultimately, the success of every student.

3

SCHOOLS AS THE CENTER OF COMMUNITIES

Significant progress is being made to connect schools and communities to improve the achievement of students. A school as the center of community is an idea that is increasingly accepted. A great number of these community schools help to articulate the research devoted to ways that communities can make better use of their school facilities and how schools and communities can work together. The federal 21st Century Community Learning Centers program enacted in 1998 is now funded at $1 billion and is a tremendous incentive in building school and community partnerships.

Decker and Decker (2000) consider the definition of community as the essential first step in understanding and cooperating with the community. They make a salient point that often gets lost in the research and ideas to repair ailing schools and systems: "educational problems reflect community and family problems in all of their complexity, diversity, and intractability" (13). Every community is different and to try and find a "one size fits all" approach to defining community can be daunting. Dwyer (1998) suggests that community is a group of people who are socially independent, who participate together in discussion and decision making, and who share certain practices that both define community and are nurtured by it. The overarching theme of community as it exists within the context of public education is that steps must be taken to reconnect the public to public education. Community education and the notion of community-based schools is a proven process for building communities and involving families in the education of their children (Decker and Boo 1998).

The vision for community education and community schools must contain a concise explanation of a community school. The best description of a community school comes from the Coalition for Community Schools.

> A community school is both a place and a set of partnerships where an integrated focus on academics, services, supports and opportunities leads to improved student learning, stronger families and healthier communities. Using public schools as a hub, community schools knit together inventive, enduring relationships among educators, families, community volunteers, and community partners—businesses, family support groups, health and social service agencies, youth development organizations, community organizations, and other organizations—committed to children. They act in concert to transform traditional schools—permanently—into partnerships for excellence. Because individual schools and the school system join forces with community agencies and organizations to operate community schools, schools are not left to work alone. (Blank, Melaville, and Shah 2003, 2)

Most important when considering the idea of community schools is to understand that the notion of connecting schools with communities and resources is not another initiative to be completed and checked off an ever-growing "to do" list. The essence of community education is to understand that it is a new lens and a new way of thinking and viewing how public education can meet the ever demanding needs of a changing populace and succeed in educating all students. By connecting and establishing processes that include communities and community-based agencies, schools can begin to assist family engagement with school in a whole new light.

THE ADVANTAGES OF COMMUNITY SCHOOLS

The Coalition for Community Schools and groups like it understand the advantages of community-based educational opportunities. Being able to build a better and stronger capacity for helping students achieve at their highest levels is at the core of why educators need to embrace the concept of community schools. Involving communities provides access to additional resources and opportunities for school environments and programs that meet the needs of all students, not just some students. Developing students in an academic venue has been a core process of public education from its inception. A community school not only develops academic proficiencies but inspires students to learn and grow in nonacademic venues as well. This marriage produces the landscape within which all students can learn at high levels. Lastly, the idea of social capital, reinforced and enhanced by connecting students to the community, is now a source of learning and exploration.

COMMUNITY PARTNERSHIPS VS. COMMUNITY SCHOOLS

Of late, the idea of business and community partnerships is sometimes seen as a substitute for the central idea of schools as community learning centers. Many schools have business and community partnerships and are encouraged to broaden these relationships by local school boards and educational foundations that have been created to support such relationships. Even though these partnerships are encouraged and quite common in public schools, they lack direction, mission, and vision to achieve the goals set for the alliance. These partnerships, many induced by schools and some by businesses and community agencies themselves, are well meaning and have the best interests of students at heart, but fall short of connecting the tenets of the partnership to student learning and outcomes.

The idea of community school contains an "informed expectation that partners will contribute to achieving specific results. . . . Partners understand that their contributions must help fulfill the conditions for learning and demonstrably connect to the school's agenda rather than diverting attention from it" (Blank et al. 2003, 7).

COMMUNITY SCHOOLS AND SOCIAL CAPITAL

The idea of social capital is a good way to begin to explore and consider our civil society. Before launching into a discussion of social capital and its relevance to community schools and family engagement, it seems logical to determine what exactly social capital means. One of the best descriptions comes from Robert Putnam, author of *Bowling Alone: America's Declining Social Capital.*

> Whereas physical capital refers to physical objects and human capital refers to the properties of individuals, social capital refers to connections among individuals—social networks and the norms of reciprocity and trustworthiness that arise from them. In that sense social capital is closely related to what some have called "civic virtue." The difference is that "social capital" calls attention to the fact that civic virtue is most powerful when embedded in a dense network of reciprocal social relations. A society of many virtuous but isolated individuals is not necessarily rich in social capital. (Putnam 2000, 19)

Interaction enables people to build communities and, more importantly, commit themselves to each other. A sense of belonging can bring great benefit to all people. In the case of building learning communities, students, teachers, parents, and community members at large all benefit from the collaboration that promotes social capital. Social capital shapes child development. Trusting and meaningful relationships coupled with reciprocity within and among those who inhabit schools and those who do not (family, peers, community) have a powerful effect on student opportunities, choices, and ultimately, their behaviors and choices. If financial capital helps people buy things, then social capital helps people to obtain their needs by increasing connections to networks of people and information. For students, investing in the concept of social capital and community education helps to define goals and dreams, develops powerful relationships with role models, and gives students the necessary information to understand the unending options that life has to offer.

WHAT IS A COMMUNITY LEARNING CENTER?

In his book *Transforming Schools into Community Learning Centers,* Steve Parson presents a concise explanation of a community learning center and also discusses the components found within them. Community learning centers can be developed from any existing school or built from the ground up. The components of the community learning center include services for the whole community in addition to the regular education of children. Community resources become a natural extension and regular part of the instructional program. Services for families and children work together to provide needed programs and services. All facets of the community can garner access to technology, and leadership is shared among all of the community stakeholders.

In cities like Sacramento, Cleveland, and Chicago, community and educational leaders have made a commitment to support and develop community learning centers. Mayor Daley of Chicago, for example, has made a long-term commitment to transform 100 schools into community centers with extended hours. In addition to numerous community organizations, foundations such as the Mott, Ford, Wallace, and Kettering also are pledging resources to these projects.

Many school officials fear that the lack of funding and strict guidelines imposed by the No Child Left Behind federal legislation may result in large numbers of schools being labeled as low performing. This federal legislation will lead to a rising demand for more learning time for hundreds of thousands of children, which will place educators under pressure to create more after-school learning opportunities. Some educators may feel that these opportunities should be limited to math and reading to raise test scores and, in the process, eliminate enrichment programs like the arts and music. This focus on test scores and standards may force educators to see little gain by investing time and energy in school and community partnerships, or ignore them altogether.

The landscape of public education is changing. Cities and states across the country are in fiscal distress and struggling to balance budgets. There may be, however, a silver lining to these problems. School and municipal leaders may be much more open to the idea that they will be able to find economies and save money by combining resources and building schools as community learning centers.

There also exists the notion that schools as community learning centers can also assist students and their families with physical, mental, and emotional health needs. Comprehensive school-based health care helps improve attendance, behavior, and grades. Mental health services contribute to better school performance and an improved school climate as well as increased self-confidence. Proper nutrition and physical exercise have significant impact on student academic outcomes and participation in school as well as on psychosocial functioning (Blank et al. 2003).

To begin to address the academic needs of students, educational leaders must consider the noninstructional influences that are predominate in those areas outside of the classroom and how a healthy and productive relationship with the community in creating community-based schools will ultimately support the mission of all schools. When schools are designed and constructed to be community schools or learning centers, opportunities for students increase in instructional and noninstructional areas. Family involvement and engagement with school and their children's academic programs increase and a sense of responsibility by families, for their children's learning, improves. The relationships of all constituencies within schools and communities strengthen and communities become stronger and more vibrant.

MAPPING COMMUNITY ASSETS

No discussion of connecting the community with schools and developing community learning centers would be complete without a discussion of community asset mapping. Asset mapping surveys the individual capabilities within a community. These assets are noted and recorded, and then mapping moves to the next level, association or organization mapping. This venture develops a list of community-based and citizen associations and nonprofits and what each can offer families and schools. The next step of this process is institutional mapping. Information is collected and cataloged about institutions, which includes businesses, government agencies, and local city, county, or regional services.

Asset mapping is a philosophy pioneered by John P. Kretzman and John L. McKnight in their book *Building Communities from the Inside Out: A Path toward Finding and Mobilizing a Community's Assets*. The authors identify two different paths for supporting communities. The first path focuses on a community's needs, deficiencies, and problems. The second path is quite different in that it begins with a clear commitment to discovering a community's capacities and assets. It is this second vision that most supports the notion of community learning centers and community education.

Community asset mapping is an inventory of those individuals, associations, organizations, and institutions that not only provide services to the community at large but, as an inventoried collection of assets, can assist schools in providing important information to families as well as establishing important relationships with the various facets of the community.

Schools who wish to begin the process of community asset mapping should begin by forming a comprehensive team that reflects the diversity of the school and community. A process for mapping communities appears in chapter 9.

THE MARKETING OF SCHOOLS

As educators, we often do not consider concepts that are not traditionally associated with education; marketing is one such concept. Educational leaders are not schooled in marketing and often do not understand this aspect of their role as school and community leader. In fact, each day as students leave our schools, as teachers discuss issues with parents and community in formal and informal situations, as newsletters are published, as media attention is focused on education in the form of test scores and as school grades are publicized, and as the political landscape changes to continue to increase the standards we have for our children, the concept of educational marketing has never been more important.

The importance of marketing in education has increased due to changing paradigms in communities, education, and society. The number of people without children in the public schools has grown. These voters will not support higher taxes for education or educational programs unless they have information about the advances in education. The very existence of accountability suggests that collaboration and communication within and among key constituents is important in supporting public education. If the goal of educators is to increase parent engagement and promote that engagement through community-based associations, then the need to market this concept is essential to success. As our economy waxes and wanes, school budgeting forces school leaders to make sure they promote the ideals, successes, and needs of their schools in an appropriate and convincing manner. Carroll and Carroll (1994) suggest that some of the characteristics of smart schools include a focus on retaining community support and information that is issued regularly and professionally.

FAMILIES THAT ARE THE COMMUNITY

Even though much demographic and community research points to an increasing number of people who do not have children in public schools, focusing on those families who do and the organizations and institutions to which they are connected is an important first step in building a strong community base and transforming a school into a community school.

Many parents work. Many families are members of community organizations and activities. Families with small children can often be found on soccer fields and dance recitals. Many families who live and work in the community are members of local organizations such as the Kiwanis, Rotary, and other similar organizations. Using all of these community organizations as a pathway for connecting a school to the community is logical when families who are connected to your school are connected to the institutions or organizations.

Local corporations and business interest in schools can be increased when employees who are involved in the schools put forward ideas, information, and proposals on behalf of the school. Neighborhood organizations, such as home boards and soccer clubs, are all filled with those families who have children attending the school. Highlight these assets and use them to make headway in building a community school.

THE ROLE OF TECHNOLOGY IN FAMILY PARTNERSHIPS

Technology provides only an opportunity; an active interest on the school's part in increasing parental involvement is necessary if the opportunity is to be used.

—James Coleman

Technology can significantly bolster the partnerships between home and school provided school leadership understands the value in strong family partnerships. Students can also attain the autonomy in their education and accountability for learning, which is essential to long-term success.

With the advent of technological applications in education, school leaders have new resources at their disposal. Blanchard (1997) explains how technology can serve the family–school connection: (1) communication and information, (2) learning and instruction, (3) interest and motivation, and (4) resources and costs. He expands on these four areas by highlighting specific technological applications: establishing two-way communication between homes and schools; discussing school experiences within and among families and communities; involving families who are presently difficult to reach; helping teachers and families acquire needed knowledge and skills; building the capacity of the schools to improve the educational health of the family; helping parents extend learning to the home in more meaningful ways by allowing them to be instructors or coaches as well as learning partners; helping families and schools motivate children; providing support and coordination for homes and schools to sustain involvement; and reducing resource costs of educating children.

VOICE-MAIL APPLICATIONS

The first schoolwide application of voice-messaging technology was in 1987. Experiments resulted in the Transparent School Model, which could be used in any school (Bauch 1997). The model provides voice-based information between teachers and parents and has at its core two primary functions: First, parents can call and listen to the teacher's daily message; and second, the system can send automated calls to parents with information that the families need. In most schools the results are astonishing. At least half of the parents call every day to hear teacher messages. Parent involvement rates go up by 500–800 percent. Student learning performance goes up and success rates improve (Bauch 1997). New technology can now link the voice-messaging system with the school's web page, allowing Internet access to the same school and class information as well as attendance and achievement data for individual students.

Voice mail, e-mail, interactive websites, and other two-way communication systems are now established ways to open schools to virtually all homes. But it is the telephone that continues to have all the advantages of familiarity, easy use, and widespread availability. In order for schools to be successful with using technology to promote true parent involvement, rather than defaulting to a more traditional, one-way "homework hotline" communications approach, teacher training and the personal involvement of the individual school's leader are critical to long-term success.

A logical step in the lineage of voice-messaging applications was the creation of the Bridge Project. Funded by the American Business Collaboration and in partnership with Vanderbilt University, schools across the country had the opportunity to apply for grant funding to install voice-messaging technology as a way to garner more parent involvement with school. In 1995, 104 schools successfully completed grants and were funded for the Bridge Project. Before starting the Bridge program, the mean number of parent contacts per teacher per day for Bridge Project schools was 2.66. Only two to three parents had any type of interaction with their child's teacher on any given day; most parents had none. After one month of using the voice-messaging technology, in tandem with concepts learned from Transparent School Model training, parent contacts per teacher per day increased to 11.46. This initial gain was about 430 percent. As more schools reported data, the figure rose to 487 percent. When adding messaging and actual contacts together, the overall increase in parent involvement is almost 500 percent. The range of increase of Bridge Project schools was from 236 percent to 950 percent. There is also correlation between the effort a school placed on publicity to promote its new technology and the frequency of system use.

Principals adapting the "five types" method of publicity (that is, promoting the system five different ways) were more successful in attaining high usage rates. The "five-type" system includes the three major categories of written, aural, and verbal communication. Under these headings there exist ideas such as newsletters, magnetized memo pads, pencils, signs, buttons, banners, feature stories, student projects depicting the event or practice, and so forth. The point made is a simple one: the more diversity in communicating your ideas, the more likely families and communities will comprehend the message and participate in the program being promoted.

Stonewall Jackson High School acted as a pilot school for the Bridge Project. Baseline data collected at the school before the Bridge Project implementation showed that the average rate of parent involvement was 1.3 contacts of all types per teacher per day. In the first month of project operation, there were 11,518 calls to the school. This represented 9.0 calls per teacher per day. Based on this data, there was a 592 percent increase in parent/teacher contacts, with approximately 50 percent of the school's families contacting the school daily.

The initial use of technology to promote family partnerships that incorporated telephone-based programs was later expanded to use Internet-based applications in tandem with the original concept of voice-mail messaging. Parents can access the system with a personalized password to retrieve information about their child's cumulative grades, completed and missing assignments, and class attendance. Parents can listen to voice-mail messages about classroom work through their computers while perusing this grade and attendance information. Parents have the opportunity to e-mail specific teachers or send general e-mails to the school.

HOW TECHNOLOGY REMOVES BARRIERS

There is a recurring problem that can be addressed succinctly within the context of the applications of technology to promote the engagement of all families. Even though there are years of research supporting the notion that family involvement and engagement improves the academic achievement of children, family engagement continues to be relinquished to subsidiary priority lists of educators. Engaging families is seen as important, but barriers to that engagement make it difficult—and in many cases, impossible—to develop and implement strong family engagement programs. Technology, however, does provide a systemic solution to many of the barriers that plague the efforts of educators to promote strong family engagement in their schools. To understand how technology can help, it is important to understand what the barriers are.

Research suggests that the largest barrier to family engagement is time. Families of all kinds are finding it more and more difficult to manage families and careers. Many families indicate they have little time for their children and even less time to involve themselves in their children's school life. This is especially true in single-parent families or other families in which there is one parent, guardian, or family member responsible for children. The majority of two-parent households find both mother and father working outside of the home, leaving available time at a premium.

Schools find dwindling attendance at meetings, conferences, and other school events and quickly assume that apathy exists among the families. There is nothing further from the truth. Time and long lists of responsibilities force families to make difficult choices; attending school events and being involved with their child's school life often drop on the list of priorities. It stands to reason that anything schools can do to assist parents in gathering information and monitoring their children's school development will be welcomed and appreciated by all families. Technology provides such a vehicle. Voice-mail applications and information coupled with web-based systems that provide basic information about student academic progress and attendance allow parents and families to monitor school activities at a convenient time during their schedule. Listening to messages from teachers about class happenings and assignments gives families the information they need to have discussions with their children regarding expectations. All of this makes monitoring children much easier as the barrier of time no longer stands between the home and school.

Culture is the second largest barrier to family engagement. Often, non-English-speaking families are intimidated or unsure of the school environment and are unclear as to how to gather information. Add to this idea that many of these families are socioeconomically disadvantaged, and becoming engaged with school is an impossibility. Technology allows for messages and information to be retrieved by families in an arena of security within their homes. Messages can be broadcast and sent in native languages, allowing these families the opportunity to learn about school events. This type of communication sends a distinct message to families that the school cares about them and wishes them to be engaged. This message resonates loudly among non-English-speaking communities.

The third largest barrier to family engagement is parental and family uncertainty. Adults responsible for children often had negative experiences as a child and have imposed those experiences and attitudes onto their children. Families who are uncertain are less likely to be involved with school, attend school events, or monitor their children's progress. Families who are skeptical of a school or who, for whatever reason, are negative or distrusting of a school seem to only be involved when there is a problem with their child, often siding with their child and making it difficult for the school to establish positive relationships.

Providing a technological solution to these types of families eliminates the barrier of uncertainty because they can engage in "invisible involvement." Providing technological solutions to family engagement enhances the probability that these parents and families will monitor their students and this ability may increase the likelihood of schools establishing more positive relationships.

Other barriers of school size, location, curriculum, adolescence, number of teachers, and peer relationships also provide unique challenges to educators. Technology can cut through these barriers as well. If families cannot get to the school because of transportation, technology allows them to stay involved. Teachers leaving messages designed to help families understand instructional concepts help to relieve problems associated with curriculum. As children grow older and become more independent, they are less likely to be friendly to the idea of their parents' and families' physical presence and involvement with school. Technology becomes a wonderful resource for parents who wish to teach and respect their child's independence yet stay current in their educational lives.

DETERMINING APPROPRIATE TECHNOLOGY

With numerous products on the market and a growing number of websites catering to school communication needs, determining how to select appropriate technology that will truly enhance the relationship between home and school becomes an important and significant step in building family engagement programs and practices. Understanding family engagement research, demographic data, and some technology knowledge should be coupled with a keen sense of the needs of one's own community.

Research clearly establishes a need for family involvement in the educational lives of children. Much of that research points to the need of frequent and two-way communication between homes and schools and points to time, culture, curriculum, parental uncertainty, and issues of trust as barriers that need to be breached in order to create effective home–school relationships that support all children.

An important aspect of understanding the use of technology is the notion that more technology is not necessarily better in establishing two-way and frequent opportunities for communication. The salient issue is the degree of access to technology available to the community that surrounds the school and how best to establish communication with families. With the growing popularity of cell phones, the telephone continues to be the most popular technology available to the largest population in any given community and should be a central component when determining how to use technology to promote family engagement. Even with the explosion of the Internet and e-mail, telephone technology remains the best way to connect with all families. Designing a technology system that is accessible to everyone, every day, twenty-four hours per day, 365 days per year, is the advantage that no other means of home–school communication can offer.

FAMILIES, TEACHERS, AND THE TELEPHONE

At some time during every teacher's career, he or she sets a goal of making positive phone calls to or improving direct communication with parents. Although these goals are noble, they very often are not attained. The vast majority of teachers do not have access to a phone in their classrooms and, as a result, connecting with a teacher by telephone is very difficult for parents and families. It is as difficult for teachers to gain access to telephones to make or return phone calls. Often, a series of messages and callbacks play out over a series of days, until both parties are frustrated about their lack of ability to communicate. Administrators should do all they can to provide telephones in every classroom. This step alone will revolutionize the ability for educators to communicate with their external customers. It is also important to provide educationally designed voice-mail systems to further enhance the ability for teachers and families to communicate.

The concept of schools providing "homework hotlines" is not a new one. Using voice-mail technology to leave homework assignments is a popular use of technology. Expanding the use of this concept to include information to parents about class activities, upcoming assignments, and how they can support their child's learning at home is an easy and effective way to improve the use of voice mail for those schools that have operative homework hotlines.

A typical "homework hotline" message might be: "Tonight's homework for algebra I is chapter 1, pages 13 15. All students need to know the order of operations." Even though this is a perfectly acceptable use of technology to simply list the homework assignment, it does little to include families in the varying aspects of children's school experience. The following message, designed for parents, includes them in the process of their child's education:

Hi. I am Mr. Smith, your child's period 2 algebra I teacher. Today is Monday, September 15th. We are working on the order of operations and tonight's homework is on pages 13–15 and should take twenty to thirty minutes to complete. The order of operations is a very important concept that all students need to know to continue to be successful in algebra this year. Parents, ask your children what the order of operations is; they should answer: multiplication, division, addition, and subtraction. Perhaps when you were in school the teacher helped you remember this by giving you the phrase, my dear Aunt Sally. We are having a quiz on Friday and when you call back I will tell you how that quiz went and what we will be doing next. If there is anything that I need to know about your child, please press the pound sign and leave me a message.

This message, which takes about a minute to record, provides insight into what the class is studying and how families can reinforce learning at home.

It is also arguably more information than families would usually get about any aspect of their child's school day. Most importantly, it allows families to leave a message for the teacher with information about their children. It is essential that parents have the ability to leave messages directly for their child's individual teachers. Some systems allow for messages to be sent to a central location rather than directly to individual teachers in individual classroom "mailboxes."

The ability for parents and families to leave messages for teachers is important. Often, teachers can incorporate the approximate length of time homework should take and can invite parents to leave messages if their child spent to little or too much time. Also, it is a wonderful way for parents and families to give teachers information that will help the teacher work with the child. This concept is highlighted by the following story:

A classroom teacher arrived at school one day and even though her daily ritual of preparation included checking voice mails, the teacher had other things to tend to and decided to check voice-mail messages later in the day. With the opening bell, the students filed into the classroom. One of the students, who was very rarely a problem for this teacher, arrived to his class and put his head down on the desk. After several attempts to engage the student, the teacher demanded that the student raise his head and participate in class. The student refused and continued to keep his head down. Frustrated, the teacher warned the student that further noncompliance would mean a discipline referral and removal from class. With that, the student stood up, knocking his chair over, grabbed his book bag, and stormed from the room muttering his lack of caring about whatever action the teacher would choose. It took several minutes to calm the class and refocus attention back on the lesson.

At the conclusion of the day and after the teacher wrote a discipline referral about the student earlier in the day, she finally checked her voice mail. There was one message that came in at midnight from the mother of the young man with whom she had difficulty earlier in the day. The message from the young man's mother alerted the teacher to the death of the beloved family dog. The mother went on to explain that all of the children had been up late crying, very upset about this situation, and that it seemed to affect her son the most, since he was the oldest and was just a toddler when the family got the dog. The boy and the dog were inseparable and the last night was the first night in eleven years that the dog had not slept on her son's bed. Even though she encouraged her son to stay home, he insisted on going to school so that he would not miss his first class. The mother concluded the message by informing the teacher of where she could be reached should her son not be performing well in school. She indicated that she would come and pick her son up if the situation warranted. She thanked the teacher for her understanding and concluded the message.

What would the classroom situation have been like had the teacher listened to her voice-mail message before the beginning of the school day? Would she have approached the difficult student a bit differently? Hopefully, the answers to these questions are obvious and showcase the importance of technology allowing for two-way communication between home and school.

PUBLIC ACCESS TO SCHOOL INFORMATION

In addition to the important aspect of families having direct access to their children's teachers is the notion that the school must provide a great deal of information to the general public. Most consumers are accustomed to voice-mail systems that provide a menu of options for information. The same concept can be used for school information as well. It is important for school administrators to determine the kind of information that families want to know and that is helpful to families. Decisions have to be made to limit the options so callers do not become frustrated with an endless list of options. All systems should be designed to allow callers to input selections at any time, rather than listening to entire menus. Repeat callers do not need menus.

The following list of information is provided for administrators to consider in creating public information lines. The lines can be changed based on the time of year and the importance of the information. For example, enrollment and registration information is perhaps more important in the summer months than it is during the school year.

Public Information Topics

School hours; administrators' names, voice mailbox numbers; principal's message; guidance and counseling information; sports and activities schedules and

updates; community service and support information; fund-raising information; meetings and events calendars; PTA or other parent organization information; testing information and tips on testing; unusual event or circumstance
information; tip line information; emergency information; and a directory of
voice mailboxes that can be accessed by keying letters of the staff members' last
names.

For every one of these suggested public information lines, there are numerous others that can be added. When marketed and advertised to the
community, the use of the system increases and calls that need to be fielded
by secretaries or other employees decreases. The availability of this information twenty-four hours a day is also very accommodating to all schedules and
greatly appreciated by families and the community at large.

Outbound Calling

Outbound dialing systems that can place attendance or general message calls
are as common as homework hotlines. These dialers are usually inexpensive
and provide a good way to mass-communicate important information. The
drawback of these dialing systems seems to be centered on the limited messages that can be sent and are usually limited to one location or one person
being able to set up the outbound calling system, thus constricting the potential uses of the system.

Outbound dialing should be a feature that is open to all staff members
who have voice mailboxes on the system. When teachers, coaches, activities
advisors, band directors, and other personnel all have outbound dialing capability, the opportunities to communicate are endless. Additionally, there
should be a capability to create permanent and temporary "call groups" that
can receive messages. A coach may establish a permanent call group of all
team members, while a classroom teacher may wish to set up a temporary or
one-time call group of students who might be struggling in a particular class.
With this kind of flexibility, the opportunity to communicate grows exponentially. The following story demonstrates the usefulness of this type of
communication.

A marching band director took the band to a competition. Because the
contest ran late and the band members had demanded a fast-food stop,

the buses would be arriving at school almost two hours after the scheduled time. The band director, not wanting to face a parking lot full of angry parents, stopped at a pay phone and recorded a message to the marching band call group, indicating the new arrival time of the band. Within minutes, the message was being received in the homes of band members. Parents were able to stay at home and not worry about the late arrival of the buses.

This ability to communicate and share important information creates positive feelings and trust between parents and teachers and promotes the image of a caring school.

Another important aspect of outbound calling features is the ability to send messages in multiple languages. While there is no technology yet available that automatically translates a message, there are systems that allow for messages to be recorded in different languages and, using the student management system, match the first language of the family to the appropriate message language. Simply put, families for whom Spanish is the primary language can receive an outbound message in Spanish as long as there was a message recorded in Spanish. Using the ethnicity code or other data available on the student management system makes this an easy process when the telephone and voice-mail system has the capability.

The last function of a successful outbound calling system is the ability for the system to leave messages on voice mail and answering machines, determine completed calls and hang-ups, and have the ability to be programmed to continue placing a call to a number that does not answer. Better quality systems provide a printout of successfully completed calls and any problems that the system experiences while trying to place the calls.

LINKING THE TELEPHONE TO THE INTERNET

Futurists continue to predict that we are not far from the time when all Americans will have access to the Internet in their homes, cars, televisions, and PDAs. For some, the future is already here; for others, the concept remains an Orwellian fantasy. Internet connectivity and operability has made its way to the majority of schools in the United States. More and more school districts and individual schools have posted websites with a large amount of good information for web visitors.

As familiar a tool as the Internet is to those who are computer and web savvy, it is not yet a means of communication for many, especially those who are non-English speakers and those whose socioeconomic status does not allow them the luxury of a home computer with World Wide Web access. It is difficult to estimate the percentage of the American public that has access to computers and more difficult yet to determine the access to the Internet. The degree to which a particular community has access to Internet technology varies greatly from almost no family having access to all families having access. School leaders need to determine Internet access capabilities within their own communities to get accurate information.

There are numerous products available to schools that use the Internet to bring information to parents and families. Grades, assignments, and attendance information are the most popular, with lunch information, transportation information, or other individual student data also gaining in popularity. However, this information remains out of reach for those families who do not have access to the Internet. The key to solving this problem is to find the technology that provides the same information in a voice-digitized fashion so that families can retrieve it via the telephone.

The challenge to school leaders is to find a computer-based system that allows for both a telephone-based voice-mail system as well as an Internet-based system with voice-digitization capacity to allow for Internet information to be retrieved by telephone.

THE TECHNOLOGY SOLUTION

School leaders should conduct extensive evaluations of the available technology that promotes school–family engagement. The technology system chosen should be one that is developed solely for educational use and not a system that was adapted to education from the business world. The company providing the product should be well versed in the educational needs of schools and families and should be able to demonstrate how their product reflects appropriate research and practice within schools and school districts. The successful product should have the ability to be accessed by both phone and Internet;

ease of use, both by school staff and parents, should be a high priority. The system should also have features that allow families to set thresholds for information delivery and decide the best way information should be communicated.

Each school and school district has different communities, and within those communities, families with different needs. The overarching principle in selecting technology that will best enhance family–school relationships is for school leaders to understand that technology is not the sole answer or response to issues of family engagement, and that whatever choice is made, it becomes a logical step in a sequence of efforts by the school to promote more harmony and interaction between students, their families, and schools.

THE EFFECTS OF TECHNOLOGY ON FAMILY ENGAGEMENT

Stonewall Jackson's programs of family involvement are most noticeable when analyzing the interaction of students and parents and the school's technology system, and are by far the most far-reaching of the school's efforts to promote family interaction with the academic lives of their children.

Students perceive their parents' ability to acquire this information on a regular basis as a positive aspect of being involved with school but students sometimes suffer negative repercussions of parents seeing poor grades or missed assignments. The use of technology has helped to change parental perceptions of the school. Students admit that the system has helped them to improve their levels of achievement, but readily admit they do not like the fact that their parents have access to this type of information at regular intervals throughout the year. The ease of use of the system benefits students and motivates them to stay current. Students report that parents use the system frequently and in many cases, the system is the stimulus for the educational dialogue between families and their children.

CONCLUSION

The involvement of families in education for this new century will have to be both universal and frequent. To implement a computerized telecommunications system and have it be more than just a homework retrieval system, and to use all available technology to enhance family partnerships, has, at its nucleus, a belief in community-based education and a vision for student excellence. School leaders who believe that all children can learn have attached to their vision the idea that family involvement including students, while not the only conduit to academic excellence, is critical to the success of every child. School leaders who see the technological revolution sweeping American schools know it to be a strong ally in promoting strong families and strong schools. Technology can open any school in America to the homes of students. With a solid leadership, vision, collaboration, and consistent communication with every family, student, and teacher, educational leaders can foster a deeper and more meaningful association between families and schools.

COMPREHENSIVE EVALUATION FOR FAMILY ENGAGEMENT

E ven though research clearly proves that family engagement elevates the academic performance of children, there still exists a great chasm between what we know and what we do. Practitioners must know how to establish programs for families that will improve the culture of their school and the engagement and, ultimately, the academic success of their students. School leaders should make it their mission to learn as much as possible about the role of families in the academic lives of children.

The time-honored adage of "what gets measured, gets done" is a foundation that has been lacking in the development of family engagement programs. The lack of processes developed in this area demonstrates a possible rationale for the limited arena of educational practice with regard to developing meaningful family engagement programs in schools.

IMPLEMENTING FAMILY ENGAGEMENT INITIATIVES

To enhance the successful implementation of family engagement programs in schools, a five-step process was developed to assist school leaders in working through the components of a successful program implementation. Following the description of the five-step model is a graphic representation (figure 5.1) of the model, which can be used as a quick reference for school planning teams. Each of the steps is discussed below.

Awareness

Why? This perhaps is the most important and fundamental question when beginning the process of improving family engagement. It is of little benefit to educators and other school staff members to be directed to complete a process or initiative without a thorough understanding of why the process or initiative is important or relevant to the process of learning and student achievement.

Educational leaders should take great care in designing professional development opportunities that address the correlations between engaged families and academically successful students. Teachers and school staff need to see the benefits, not only to students but to themselves as well. This process of building awareness for the concept is essential as a primary necessity for any attempt to build a successful family engagement program. Omitting this step almost always assures that the initiative will be misunderstood, poorly received, and short-lived. Helping all stakeholders become aware of the importance of this initiative is necessary to garner any consensus from staff to move forward.

Self-Assessment

To continue with the process after awareness, a school or district must take great care in assessing the degree to which they are "family friendly." The vast majority of this chapter is dedicated to the construction of a team of people to carry out this evaluation, how that team should work together, and the comprehensive evaluation itself. It cannot be emphasized enough that a fundamental step at this level is to garner the opinions and perceptions of a wide cross section of constituents and stakeholders. Much more detail regarding this concept appears in the section entitled "Involving All Constituents in Evaluation."

Program Conceptualization and Development

There is a pitfall to avoid when working through the process of initiating family engagement programs: having no concept of how or why families should be involved with their children's school. Assuming that the "why" portion of this equation is dealt with during the initial stage of awareness, the "how" then becomes the catalyst for conceptualizing and developing a family engagement plan. Discussions among educators should begin with questions such as (1) How do we wish parents and families to be involved? (2) What are the primary and secondary goals of promoting family engagement? (3) How do we envision the role of families in our school? These questions, and others, help school leaders begin the process of conceptualizing the structure of family engagement initiatives.

In tandem with the conceptualization of initiatives is the need to set policy, create attainable and measurable goals, and create workable plans to reach the goals set forth in the plan. Appropriate procedures to accomplish these tasks appear throughout the remainder of the chapter. Ultimately, school leaders should develop a guiding plan to begin the process of infusing families within the educational lives of their children.

Program Implementation

Schools that follow the outline through this step will undoubtedly generate numerous ideas to be implemented. Be wary of trying to implement too much, too fast. It is advisable to pilot programs or phase in plans over months or years. Beginning with a full, simultaneous implementation of all ideas and facets of family engagement will lead to certain failures within the program and may cause dissention among teachers and erode the trust of families in communities. It is better to do a small project well than a large project poorly.

School leaders and teams charged with implementing family engagement programs can reap tremendous benefits from resources already available within the school and community. Chapter 9 and the appendix have procedures and ideas for collecting and mapping school and community assets.

Family engagement program initiatives include the "3 Ps": policies, procedures, and practices. Including and engaging families in schools is an important component of an overall scheme to improve the culture of a school. Remember, what people believe, value, and how they interact are all important facets of changing a school culture. Keeping the "3 Ps" in mind can help to ensure that culture change takes place, making initiatives more likely to be permanent rather than fleeting.

Evaluating and Sustaining

Perhaps the most challenging of the five steps is the last one: evaluating the programs and sustaining the energy necessary to allow the initiatives to become part of the culture of the school. Because this step is the most difficult in any process, it is often overlooked, omitted, or ignored. The consequences that result from a lack of evaluation of effort and ideas to sustain programs are dire. In most cases, the entire project fails. Initial enthusiasm gives way to complacency and complacency leads to failure. To avoid this, school leaders are strongly encouraged to have mechanisms in place to use the available data and research to evaluate and sustain initial efforts in family engagement.

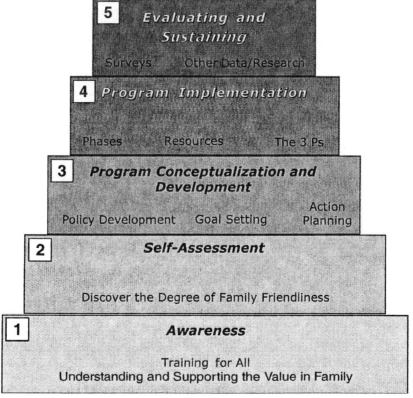

Figure 5.1. The Family Friendly School's Five-Step Model for Implementing Family Engagement Initiatives

Surveys, focus groups, student data, etc., can all be used to continue the forward momentum of family engagement programs.

INVOLVING ALL CONSTITUENTS IN EVALUATION

In order to create measurable goals for family engagement, the need for a comprehensive analysis is essential. The best manner in which to analyze programs, practices, policies, procedures, and the school environment itself is to participate in a thorough and comprehensive evaluation of the degree to which these items are conducive to family engagement with school.

Most evaluation documents are developed in response to a perceived need. An assessment of family engagement in a school or school district should be a process that involves the systematic collection, analysis, and integration of information. Assessment is central to the educational process and provides data that, in turn, helps to identify needs and, ultimately, responses to those needs. Responsive evaluation also must emphasize feedback from all sources.

The comprehensive evaluation for family engagement that appears in this chapter is designed to provide important information and feedback with regard to several components of effective family engagement programs. Included are the areas of school environment, processes to engage all families, community outreach, and the encouragement of student engagement and its relationship to family engagement with school. Essential to this process is the idea of ensuring that the evaluation is responsive and includes the ideas and opinions of all whom the school serves.

In undertaking this process of evaluation, a committee should be formed that will work together from beginning to end to provide for a consistent set of responses to the questions asked. First and foremost, the committee must include the leader, whether that is the principal of a school or a superintendent of a school district. The participation of the leader, and not his or her designee, signifies that the assessment is indeed important and that results and needs will be a component of the mission and direction of the organization.

In addition to the leader, there should be a cross section of school staff to include various curricular areas as well as support staff membership. The diversity of a school's staff should be reflected in those who participate on this committee. This may mean that staff members who are reluctant to participate in activities such as a working committee must be convinced that their perceptions are important to the work of the committee. School leadership should look for a wide variety of people, interests, and attitudes. The attitudes and opinions of secretaries, teacher aides, security staff, cafeteria workers, bus drivers, and custodians are also extremely important when discussing and evaluating the engagement of families. This variety of employees brings about the best opportunity for rich data collection.

The second significant component of the committee should be families. In a similar fashion to acquiring school staff members, effort should be made to find those families who are somewhat disenfranchised from the school. This may mean locating families who are non-English-speaking or families who have experienced difficulties with the school. Leaders must avoid the trap of assigning those parents and families who are already involved, engaged, and supportive of the school. Acquiring these types of parents will most certainly garner a positive viewpoint of the school's efforts and thus may limit the degree of effectiveness of the evaluation.

Listening to disgruntled customers and responding accordingly is a cornerstone of business operations. There is often resistance on the part of school leaders to reach out to those who have experienced problems and who may have a negative viewpoint of the school. Working on a project like improving relationships and promoting the engagement of families is a technique that very much might reengage disenfranchised or disgruntled parents. This, in turn, works in favor of the school, as parents and families discuss school initiatives in the community. Even though there may be an initial degree of uncertainty and discomfort, the end result is a positive boost for the committee and ultimately the school and its relationships with all families.

Student representation makes up the final component of the committee. The model upon which the assessment is based strongly implies that students need to be an integral component in the development of the school environment in which they learn. It is quite appropriate to include students of all ages, with the understanding that younger students who participate may have to limit participation or their participation may need to be structured in a different manner. But to not include students of any age suggests that they can offer nothing concrete to the development of a culture in which they spend a significant amount of their time. Sagor (2002) points out that humans are encouraged to invest in difficult undertakings when their desires to feel competent, to belong, to be useful, to feel potent, and to feel optimistic, are satisfied.

The same pitfalls in selecting student representatives exist as when selecting parents and family members. Care and consideration should be taken to select students who represent the breadth and depth of diversity of a particular school. Although it is acceptable to include student leaders, student participation should not be limited to student leaders who are already engaged with school and have different experiences than those students whose engagement with school and activities are limited. A great deal can be learned about why parents and families are not engaged with school from those students who are minimally engaged themselves. As Sagor (2002) so aptly reminds us, we can learn great lessons from skateboarders.

GROUP PROCESSES

Although the purpose of this book is not to teach groups of people to work together, it is important to devote some space to the importance of group process. The success of any team of people with a common mission is the degree to which all involved can actively participate and that each member of the group feels like a productive and contributing member. There are a few simple processes that can be used to make sure that the family engagement evaluation committee works as a cohesive unit.

Roles and Responsibilities within the Group

Each committee or group should have a chairperson, timekeeper, facilitator, and recorder. Brief descriptions of these roles follow.

The *chairperson* should be elected from within the committee and not be appointed or preappointed prior to the first meeting of the group. The chairperson should possess those skills that will keep the group moving forward and keep focused on the task of the comprehensive evaluation of family engagement practices.

The *timekeeper* should ensure that the meeting starts on time, ends on time, and that discussions do not go beyond prescribed timelines. At the onset of the first meeting, the timekeeper should help the group decide the meetings' times and lengths, breaks, and so forth so that all members understand how meetings will be conducted.

The *facilitator* acts as a quasi sergeant at arms. This position keeps the focus on the topic and keeps discussions from spinning off to other topics. The facilitator helps avoid sidebar and small-group conversations while the meeting is taking place. There may be times when the facilitator can rephrase or redirect the group when the discussion is bogged down with detail or disagreement. Most importantly, the facilitator should be someone skilled or trained in the art of building consensus. It may very well be up to the facilitator to help guide the group toward consensus and find the common ground that all can support.

In order to have a detailed summary of meeting happenings, all committees should have a *recorder*. In addition to taking notes, the recorder is also responsible for bringing the materials necessary for the group to be productive, such as notepaper, markers, easels, pads, tape, and so on. The recorder is responsible for collecting all the information during a meeting and preparing it in a format that can be reviewed at subsequent meetings.

Meeting Guidelines

When people agree to participate on any type of committee, they do so at significant personal expense. The time they spend with a committee could be spent with family at home; therefore, being respectful of the time that is being devoted to the committee is important to successful participation. The following meeting guidelines will ensure that the committee remains focused and productive:

1. Meetings start at the specified time.
2. Meetings are in an appropriate setting and are uninterrupted.
3. Participants are punctual and actively listen.
4. All members actively participate.
5. Participants are willing to meet consensus.
6. Participants respect the agenda.
7. Meetings end at a specified time.
8. Participants are respectful of timekeeping.

The selection process of membership to the family engagement evaluation committee will guarantee that the membership is representative of the constituency served by the school. The diversity and representativeness of the group may require a mechanism to allow for balancing the group in terms of race, sex, and other variables. It is also important to note that people may be more giving of their time when there are specific issues and a timetable that includes a target date for concluding the committee's business.

Effective committees have a clear sense of purpose that is dictated by the comprehensive evaluation of family engagement process. A clear sense of purpose guarantees a sense of fulfillment at the end of the process. Meetings should have clear agendas and be action oriented. The leadership of the committee does not necessarily have to be the principal or other school leader but can be any member of the committee who has been elected or decided by the committee.

BUILDING CONSENSUS

Building consensus considers *what* is right, not *who* is right. Consensus results when conflicting ideas and opinions are brought out and each individual is heard and understood by the group. The emotions and feelings of all committee members are appropriate to be shared, as that is a normal process that will allow members to know that their viewpoints have been heard. As the process of consensus develops, the group seeks to find better solutions or the best solutions from any that are being proposed. The key component to building consensus, however, is listening.

To determine if all group members have reached the mutual acceptance of a decision, the leader or facilitator should ask:

1. Does everyone accept the decision? An answer of yes means the decision has been made.
2. Is there any opposition to the decision? If no one speaks, the answer may be that everyone agrees with the decision; the questioner should, however, be alert for nonverbal signs, which could indicate opposition.
3. Can everyone live with the decision? A yes answer ensures that no one has a strong conflict with the decision.

Participation by All Members

The dynamics of any group almost always guarantees that there are both strong and weak personalities, which in turn ensures an uneven rate of participation. Add to this those people who may have limited English skills or be insecure by the surroundings, and the need to have processes in place that allow all to participate is obviously essential for group development and progress.

The chairperson or facilitator of the group should possess the ability to allow all committee members the opportunity to be heard. Encouraging all to participate, especially those who might be reluctant, is a key ingredient in getting the perceptions of all constituents. In addition to discussion and large-group process, the committee can be divided up into teams that, in turn, can list opinions and perceptions and then share those with the group at large.

In addition to discussions and subgroups, the ability for all members to participate includes nonverbal processes as well. For example, a question could be posed to the group on how the main office of the school could be made more "family friendly." Each group member could be given several slips of sticky notepaper and individuals could write their ideas down on the paper. Then, during a break in the meeting, they could post their responses on a board or chart paper. The facilitator could then categorize the ideas and from this, discussions and direction could be mapped. Should there be the need for clarification of a particular idea, the originator then could address the group as to the impetus of the idea or suggestion.

THE COMPREHENSIVE EVALUATION FOR FAMILY ENGAGEMENT

The first step in the process of developing family engagement programs, practices, procedures, and policies in a school is to evaluate and assess the present attention being paid to family engagement. The committee (as identified earlier in this chapter) should undertake the following evaluation. Each member of the committee should have the opportunity to respond to each question and the committee should come to a consensus as to strengths and weaknesses that exist in the school. Once complete, the evaluation acts as a needs assessment from which plans can be developed and implemented, and most importantly, evaluated.

Does Your School Say Welcome?

The school's physical appearance is important when establishing partnerships with families and community.

1. Do your school entrances welcome all families?
2. Are entrances clearly marked and understandable by all?
3. Are your faculty, student, and community parking well marked and understandable by all?
4. Is handicapped parking clearly marked?
5. Are handicapped entrances accessible and clearly marked?
6. Are the parking lots and entrances well lit?
7. If you experience graffiti at your school, is it promptly removed?
8. Is the interior of your school clean and well kept?
9. Do families perceive your school as being safe?
10. Does your school have a standing school beautification committee and does your budget include funds for such?
11. Does your school building contain understandable directional signs?
12. Is there a comfortable reception area for families?
13. Does your school have a parent or family center?
14. Is your school administration approachable by all families?
15. Does your school provide translation services for families who do not speak English?
16. Does your school minimize the use of educational jargon?
17. What family education programs does your school provide?
18. Do staff members treat families courteously?

Engaging All Families

When reviewing the level of family involvement in the educational lives of children, the school's educational programs, and the school environment, be sure to ask yourself which families are involved in the following. Are they always the same people? Remember, the lives of modern families are extremely complicated. Simplify their ability to be involved in school—they will be most appreciative of your efforts to include them and the benefits to your school will be immense.

Mission and Governance

1. In what kinds of initiatives does your school engage to promote family engagement? Be specific.
2. Does your school have a written policy or goal regarding family engagement?
3. Is family engagement incorporated into the mission of your school?
4. Are families aware of the mission and vision of your school? How have they been made aware?
5. Are family members included in staff professional development programs?
6. Are families part of the school governing council?
7. How are family members selected to be on the school governing council?
8. Are all demographic areas represented on your school council?
9. Does your school train families to participate in school governance?

Availability and Time

1. Are nonschool hours used for family conferences with staff?
2. Are school/family activities held in places other than the school (i.e., closer to certain communities)?
3. Do you promote family visitations during the school day?
4. Does your school offer families help with transportation or babysitting for scheduled events?

Two-Way Communication with All Families

1. How are families provided contact information for all staff members? Is the information accessible by *all* families?
2. Do families have telephone numbers, e-mail, and website addresses for the school and its faculty?
3. What is the school policy for teacher communication with all families?

4. Is there a policy for family communication with teachers?
5. Do all teachers communicate regularly with families?
6. How does the school assist families with understanding educational objectives?
7. How often are grade and assignment information made available to families?
8. Is curriculum information provided to all families in an easily understood, jargon-free format?
9. Does your school communicate in multiple languages?
10. Are school policies and regulations easily accessible?
11. How often does your school send a newsletter?
12. Does your school publish a calendar?
13. Are your security measures well publicized?
14. Do you provide a written profile of your school to share with students, parents, and guests?

Opportunities for Interaction

1. Does your school require conferences with all families of students?
2. Does your school require family approval of student course selections?
3. Do families have input on all program and policy changes at your school?
4. Does your school maintain an active parent/teacher/student organization?
5. Does your school encourage an active, well-defined volunteer program?

Community Outreach

Family engagement and community involvement often go hand in hand.

1. Is your school a community school?
2. Are your school facilities available for community use?
3. What types of extended-day programs exist at your school?
4. Is your school equipped to become a community learning center?

5. Does your school act as a polling place on Election Day?
6. Does your school have a website that is current and updated?
7. Are your school planning and curriculum documents available to the community?
8. How many different ways does your school publish telephone numbers, fax numbers, e-mail addresses, and website addresses for the benefit of the community?
9. Does your school have a marketing plan?
10. How many and what kinds of events are held each year that involve families and community members?
11. Have you mapped the assets available in your community?
12. Does your school have an organized public relations program?
13. How many established business and community partnerships is your school involved in?

Engaging Families with Students

Research clearly indicates that students who are not engaged in their school and their learning do not achieve at the highest possible levels. Family engagement promotes student engagement.

1. How often do you provide families information about their children's academic progress?
2. How do you provide cocurricular and athletic activities information to all families?
3. How do you promote high interest in your school by all families?
4. How do you encourage family involvement with creating enhanced home learning environments and activities?
5. How does your school promote community service activities?
6. How are your important events promoted to families and the larger community?

6

DOES YOUR SCHOOL SAY WELCOME?

Beginning with this chapter, each of the areas found within the comprehensive evaluation is restated, along with information for schools as to how to implement or improve upon existing conditions. This information is a valuable resource to school committees that begin the process of analyzing and evaluating the degree to which their school is "family friendly."

Each question within each broad topic area is restated, followed by specific information that responds to the evaluation question.

The school's physical appearance is important when establishing partnerships with families and community.

1. DO YOUR SCHOOL ENTRANCES WELCOME ALL FAMILIES?

Almost every school building in the United States has some sort of sign or door decal that either warns visitors to report directly to the main office or warns trespassers of negative consequences should they be on the school premises for any reason without proper authorization. Most schools and school districts have regulations that guide the practice of how schools accept visitors. Since many of the school shooting tragedies, these policies are not only enforced but, in many schools, visitors cannot get far beyond the front doors without proper identification, sign-in logs, visitor badges, and other requirements that ensure the safety of building inhabitants. Most communities have come to expect these processes to be in place, but there still exists the notion that this type of security should not have to be present in a school building. Even though the reality is that this type of security has become very necessary to provide an environment of safety, these types of security precautions still leave visitors uneasy. It is important that these measures not only are in place but that we remember to remain friendly to guests of the school. Asking for identification with a smile and taking the time to explain the rationale for certain school procedures helps guests understand the policies in place.

The messages that we send our guests are sometimes frightful. Very rarely are there signs that say "welcome," and even more rare are signs that say "welcome families." Supporting the premise that creating a positive school culture is essential to the achievement of all students and that family engagement is a necessary component of that culture, an evaluation of school entrances is in order. The following door decals were developed by Family Friendly Schools and were designed to not only deliver the important message of signing in but to present a welcoming feeling to those who are visiting the school.

Welcome!

Please   sign   in.

A Family Friendly School:
Where our community supports
academic achievement for all students

Bienvenidos!

Favor   de   firmar   al   entrar.

Una Escuela Abierta para la Familia
En dónde nuestra comunidad apoya el triunfro

Figure 6.1.   Welcome Signs

At Stonewall Jackson High School, the administration scraped off the old red warning signs and replaced them with the new decals. The new decals were done in blue, which is a more welcoming color than the red warning signs. Many families and guests have positively commented on the signs, both English-speaking and Hispanic/Latino parents. Similar decals can be made in any language necessary to welcome school guests.

How guests, especially families, feel upon entering a school is an important first step in building the important relationships necessary for effective family engagement programs.

2. ARE ENTRANCES CLEARLY MARKED AND UNDERSTANDABLE BY ALL?

When you arrive at Stonewall Jackson High School, you are faced with a few decisions. There are three main driveways, two huge parking lots, and three main entrances on the front of the building. Which driveway do you use? Which parking lot do you use? Which door do you use? These kinds of basic issues keep the intimidation factor high within the mind-set of families and guests. Large signs were placed outside to direct people to what are believed to be the three most popular destinations when guests visit our school: the gymnasium, the auditorium, and the office. Guest parking is clearly marked. There are also greeters at the entrances to ensure that guests can find what or who they are looking for. Additionally, pictures of administrators and guidance staff as well as building maps are available so that guests can put a name to a face as well as find their way to an office.

Whether your school is in a city, an urban setting, a congested suburban setting, or a rural setting, consider working with your city or county in placing directional signs at intersections near your school, especially if your school is hard to find. The more you can do to help your guests find your school, the happier they will be when they arrive. Student artists love the opportunity to demonstrate their talent and help the school at the same time. Discuss ideas with students and teachers about how entrances can be made more inviting and informative to all guests.

Another idea is to align outdoor markers, such as flagpoles or the school marquee, with the entrance that is most often used or the one that you would prefer guests use. It becomes easier to remind guests to enter "at the flag-pole" or "nearest the marquee." Many large schools have numerous outdoor entrances. Another idea would be to paint the entrances different colors to represent different areas of the school. Sporting events or musical events could have their own symbols and colors, making it very easy for guests to identify the appropriate entrances.

3. ARE FACULTY, STUDENT, AND COMMUNITY PARKING WELL MARKED AND UNDERSTANDABLE BY ALL?

As was stated above, parking should be clearly marked. If there is no public parking at your school, then provide written information as to where guests can park. Sometimes it is possible to enter into agreements with local businesses or parking garages to allow your guests to park at a reduced or free rate. If you have dignitaries visiting your school, save convenient parking for them so that their limited time is not spent looking for parking. Enforce the rules about students or staff not parking in guest parking. Make sure that you have enough parking spaces devoted to guests. Again, consider using different colors or different signs to designate the separate types of parking. If you have large parking lots, you might consider numbering the spaces or identifying the lot with a letter or name. If, for instance, you schedule a day for families to visit your school, consider the logistics of how they will get to your school and, if driving, where they will park.

If driving to your school is not the preferred manner, then help your guests with directions on the use of public transportation. Letting them know which subway, bus, transfer, stop, or similar marker is all part of helping guests begin their visit at your school with a positive mind-set. Publish schedules and emphasize when the first and last train or bus is available. Schedule your activities around these timetables to make family participation simpler.

4. IS HANDICAPPED PARKING CLEARLY MARKED?
5. ARE HANDICAPPED ENTRANCES ACCESSIBLE AND CLEARLY MARKED?

It often is a common practice to have hundreds and hundreds of parking spaces available at large schools and devote one or two of those spaces to handicapped individuals. Sometimes the handicapped parking is not near the handicapped entrance, as was the case at Stonewall Jackson. There were two spaces in the front of the building devoted to handicapped parking, but the handicapped access to the school was in the rear of the building. The rationale for this peculiar arrangement was due to the front of the building having two steps but the rear entrances were ground level. Since the ground-level entrances required no modifications for handicapped access, they were the designated handicapped entrances, even though parking spaces existed in the front of the building. This situation was rectified by placing a ramp and automatic door on the front entrance of the building and designating handicapped parking in the rear of the building. As a result of these improvements, each of the first-floor entrances, both front and rear, is now accessible to the disabled. Making sure that your building is accessible by handicapped guests is more than following legal guidelines. You must send a positive and distinct message that handicapped guests are welcome and that the school staff has made every effort to accommodate them.

6. ARE THE PARKING LOTS AND ENTRANCES WELL LIT?

Several years ago at a Stonewall Jackson school-based planning council meeting, a parent approached the council with concerns about outdoor lighting in the evening. She felt it was particularly dangerous to walk from the large parking lots, which were lit, to the building that was lit, but not very well. Since the school-based council meeting was in the evening, the council went outdoors to assess the situation for themselves and found the parent to be very accurate in her description. The lighting was terrible. The concrete canopy covering the main entrances and bus boarding areas were found to have none of the lights working, making the situation dark and dangerous. The council agreed that the present lighting system needed to be repaired and upgraded. All of the concrete canopy lighting was updated with halogen lighting and numerous lights were affixed to the sides of the building near all walkways. This lighting made a huge difference not only in safety but also to the appearance of the building at night. The parent was so pleased with the actions of the administration and the council that she wrote to the superintendent to express her happiness with the response of the school to her concerns. Anytime someone takes the time to write something positive is a good thing. This is a valuable lesson in customer service: find out what the needs of the customer are, then work to meet those needs.

Lighting and safety go hand in hand. There are standards in effect for appropriate outdoor lighting. Check with your local planning commission to understand the requirements of lighting and work toward meeting those requirements. Ensure that all bulbs are replaced in a timely fashion and that all exterior lighting is working. If you have a school website, perhaps parents or visitors could report nonfunctioning lights there. Set automatic timers or sensors so that lights go on at dusk and off at dawn. If finances are a problem, try working through a business partnership arrangement with your local utility company. Perhaps if the utility company were to provide funding for lights, the school could be made available to them for meetings, dinners, workshops, and similar events.

7. IF YOU EXPERIENCE GRAFFITI AT YOUR SCHOOL, IS IT PROMPTLY REMOVED?

A plan should be in place to remove graffiti from your building within twenty-four hours. Stonewall Jackson has seen one instance of graffiti in the past eight years. Spray painting and picture drawing is encouraged, but not on the building. One of the school's neighbors is a rock quarry. The quarry delivered huge rocks and placed them in strategic areas of the school property. Each of these stones "belongs" to a class or organization and they can be painted any way the class wants, provided the work is decent. School administration and security have rock patrol as part of their normal routines. The rocks come alive during homecoming spirit week when they are part of the contest to choose the spirit week winner. It is so gratifying to see all of these students (along with their parents) out by the rocks after school and on Saturdays, designing and creating new pictures and slogans. Each summer, just before school, the rocks are whitewashed and the process begins again. As long as there is a rock to paint, nobody paints the school.

Schools are encouraged to allow mural painting and to provide other areas that students can decorate to enhance the environment in which they spend so many hours. When an area is designated for this type of activity, the degree to which graffiti plagues a school is minimized. Many urban schools create large outdoor areas where graffiti artists can express themselves. Not all graffiti is bad and much of it is tremendous artwork that can instill a sense of community pride rather than community scorn. This artwork can also foster feelings of acceptance in students and families of different cultures. School administrators are encouraged to learn about "positive graffiti" and explore other opportunities for students to express themselves and have a hand in creating their own school environment.

8. IS THE INTERIOR OF YOUR SCHOOL CLEAN AND WELL KEPT?

Ancil Helton was the daytime head custodian at Stonewall Jackson High School for twenty-nine years. During Ancil's entire career at Stonewall Jackson, he witnessed the comings and goings of numerous principals. Ancil had more institutional knowledge than anyone else and loved the opportunity to share what he knew. He spoke with a fairly heavy southern accent and his speaking pace was slow and deliberate. Early in my tenure, I asked Ancil to walk with me. I complimented him on how well the building was kept up and told him that sweeping the main halls and making sure that both the interiors and exteriors of our main entrances were always monitored and well kept. There was nothing worse than having a guest come in to find a messy atmosphere, regardless of when it was. Ancil pondered my statement and surmised the following about me. "Well . . . ," he said rather slowly, "I tend to agree with ya. Ya see about three principals ago, I forget his name, but he was carin' more about the outside and didn't rightly care about the inside. Now the next, well, he was a might sticky about how the inside of the buildin' looked, but didn't rightly care about the outside all that much. Now, the one before you, I reckon he was a different sorta fella. He only cared about the path from his car to his office. But you, you are an inside-outside kinda guy."

I will forever be known as the inside-outside principal, a label I wear proudly. How the building appears to guests sends a significant message about our attitudes for an educational environment for our children and the importance we place on guests in our school.

Keeping the interior of a building well kept is important and difficult. Custodians cannot do this alone. Everyone who resides in a school building needs to take part in the appearance of a building. Classrooms need to be maintained in a neat and orderly fashion. Interior painting needs to be planned and executed so the building always looks its best. Glass doors should be wiped clean, and floors should be swept throughout the school day. The message that should be sent to guests is one of pride in building appearance. When a building is neat, clean, and orderly, regardless of its age, guests will notice—and more importantly, remember.

9. DO FAMILIES PERCEIVE YOUR SCHOOL AS BEING SAFE?

Of all of the issues with which school leaders deal, the issue of safety and security is perhaps the most prominent and most important. The word *perceive* is chosen deliberately because what people perceive is what they believe, regardless of the truth of the matter. You can have the safest most secure school in the world, but if people believe it is unsafe, then it's unsafe.

The public relations of your safety and security program are of vital importance. Work with your community and hear their attitudes and opinions. Listen to their concerns, however difficult it may be, and then take action on those concerns. When you are finished, publicize heavily the action you have taken based on community input. You might consider instituting a safety and security committee that is available to students and families to hear concerns and work collaboratively on ideas and solutions to issues.

Several years ago at Stonewall Jackson, the perception was not necessarily that the school was unsafe but that is was susceptible and prone to violence. There were concerns that at any moment something dreadful would happen. Administrators listened to several community groups talk about all kinds of security issues and then set about to create a plan to improve not only the security of our school but the perception of the school as a safe and secure environment. A video camera system was installed and the security team was extended from three to four people. Security offices were relocated and a greeter/check-in program at school entrances was established. Exterior doors were locked after the student arrival and all entrances were monitored constantly. Stonewall Jackson did not have the issues that some schools have and there was never a perceived necessity for metal detectors. However, if that were an issue, it would have been dealt with forthrightly.

A printed security and emergency plan was devised and shared with everyone. Families were informed that maintaining a safe and secure environment was a priority for our school. Most importantly, when the school does have a problem, the problem and resolution are communicated to all families as quickly and efficiently as possible. If there is an event at school that could be miscommunicated or embellished in the community, a letter goes home *that day*, in multiple languages, explaining the situation completely. Further, the telecommunications system is used to send calls home to let parents know the situation, and more importantly, know that their children are safe. It is of vital importance that you fight any urge you may have to either conceal or otherwise not represent accurately all issues within the realm of safety. Should you have an occurrence in your school and you do not report it to parents or do not report it accurately, the mistrust that will develop might never be able to be reversed. Trust that the vast majority of parents, while they may be concerned about any incident that might potentially put their child in harm's way, will welcome and appreciate your accurate and timely communication.

Making safety and security information available to the community you serve sends a clear message about your willingness to work collaboratively with all stakeholders to ensure a positive learning environment.

10. DOES YOUR SCHOOL HAVE A STANDING SCHOOL BEAUTIFICATION COMMITTEE AND DOES YOUR BUDGET INCLUDE FUNDS FOR SUCH?

How the community, families, and guests perceive the school is determined in part by the presentation of the exterior of your school. Whether your building is a year old or a hundred years old, to maintain the exterior and focus on those aspects that present it in its best light go a long way to making that all-important first impression. After many years of struggling with the upkeep of the exterior of the building, administrators at Stonewall Jackson turned the responsibility over to the Student Activities Leadership Council. The students seem to be doing the best job of anyone in maintaining and beautifying the school. If you do not have a committee, you should establish one and devote funds to it, whether they are budgeted or raised through other means. However you choose to get this accomplished is secondary to the commitment you need to make to the concept. Once again, establishing partnerships within the community can help toward this goal. Broken windows, doors, and other exterior problems should be fixed as quickly as is possible.

11. DOES YOUR SCHOOL BUILDING CONTAIN UNDERSTANDABLE DIRECTIONAL SIGNS?

Once inside Stonewall Jackson, there are four main hallways, three floors, and two visible staircases from every exterior entrance. Not only do guests have a problem navigating the building but students find it challenging as well, especially freshmen and new students who are perpetually lost for days. Stonewall has been "signed" so that one can easily flow through the halls and find the direction toward the correct destination. Room numbers, departments, names, class schedules, and so forth are all posted so that both internal and external customers can navigate the building with ease. The signs are in English and Spanish. School leaders are encouraged to go even further, adding those languages spoken at your school as well as signs in Braille.

School leaders should develop a plan so that from the minute one enters the property of the school, signs and assistance are present for all guests to find their destination with ease. It is important to remember that schools can be intimidating places for families, especially those who do not have fond memories of their own time in school. It can be more distressing for families who do not speak English. A welcoming environment is one in which any guest can be comfortable, with a welcoming atmosphere and assistance in locating any destination.

12. IS THERE A COMFORTABLE RECEPTION AREA FOR FAMILIES?

The removal of the main office counter was the first step in making a reception area that was comfortable and inviting for families and guests at Stonewall Jackson. Comfortable chairs, a receptionist, reading materials containing school information, plants, pictures of students, and similar items adorn the new reception area. When guests enter the new and improved area, they remark that the feeling one gets is not of a school office at all. It is when those comments are made that the environment is beginning to shape the positive school culture that we all desire. Reception areas are wonderful places to share positive information about your school.

13. DOES YOUR SCHOOL HAVE A PARENT OR FAMILY CENTER?

In many schools throughout the United States, the concept of parent or family centers within schools is taking hold and proving to be a valuable benefit for building lasting and effective relationships between families and schools. Family centers have a variety of characteristics, such as general support for parents, support for teen mothers, community-centered service projects, summer enrichment classes, and student remedial programs. Many non-English-speaking families utilize family centers to learn or improve English; in some schools, the center is a physical space that houses parent-oriented workshops and classes. Popular within many of the family centers is the availability of computers and Internet access for families who would otherwise not have that level of technological capability within their home.

The Institute for Responsive Education[1] concluded a study in the fall of 2002 called the High School Family Center Research Project, which was a nationwide investigation to document best practices and to identify the role of the centers as a strategy to enhance family involvement and support the successful achievement of all students. Preliminary findings of the study suggest that while the activities in these centers varied, there were common elements: a basic structure, a skilled and dedicated coordinator, and a program that supported positive student outcomes.

School leaders are encouraged to read the available research and learn about the parent and family center models that already exist and, to the degree possible, replicate those centers in their own schools. Having a space

---

[1] For more information on the Institute for Responsive Education, visit their website at www.responsiveeducation.org.

dedicated to families that provides outreach and services to enhance the educational experiences of all children is tantamount to creating the positive school culture necessary for the achievement of all students. Much of the uncertainty and intimidation that exists in many families with regard to interacting with their children's schools can be eliminated when there is a safe place for them to learn and call their own. These opportunities can only enhance relationships between families and schools. For a list of possible uses for your parent or family center, see the appendix.

14. IS YOUR SCHOOL ADMINISTRATION APPROACHABLE BY ALL FAMILIES?

Approachable means different things to different people. It is imperative that you stop and listen to anyone who wishes to speak to you at any time about any topic.

A very successful strategy for meeting families and remaining approachable is the idea of "parent coffees." Each month, find a family who is willing to host a small gathering in their home. Select different neighborhoods to make sure that over the course of one year, you have made yourself available in all neighborhoods and subdivisions. The host family announces to neighbors and friends that the principal will be available at a published time to listen to concerns, suggestions, and ideas. The host family need only provide coffee or tea. Usually ten to fifteen people come and ask questions and seek understanding of school practices, policies, and procedures. These situations are rarely (if ever) disagreeable or distressing. More often than not, families are appreciative of the opportunity to talk directly to the principal and have questions answered. If by chance a disgruntled parent attends, simply asking that parent to make an appointment to speak to you privately refocuses the event on its intended course. It is usually a relaxed atmosphere in which parents feel a sense of security, as opposed to the school or an administrative office. After participating in several of these coffees, school leaders will start to see patterns of questions. Even if the same question has been repeatedly asked, it should be answered as if it had never been asked. Families need to know that their questions are being answered in a thoughtful and serious manner. These types of outreach programs help administrators be accessible.

Another wonderful way of promoting accessibility is the practice of home visits. Many parents will not come to school no matter what you try to do. From time to time, children are suspended from school pending a parent conference. If the parent never comes in, does that mean the child never comes back to school? Home visits by administrators, counselors, social workers, and teachers are very effective in communicating important school information and sending a message to a particular family that their child is a valuable person and the school cares a great deal about his or her success. When the principal or assistant principal is knocking on a door at 10:00 A.M. on a weekday morning, families know there is an important reason. Often, it is just to establish relationships and try to break down barriers between certain families and the school. There is no stronger "I care" message than arriving at the home of a family to encourage them to be involved.

Family outreach meetings specifically designed for non-English-speaking families are also a very good way to make administrators and counselors available and accessible to families. Whether it is monthly or a few times a year, select an off-site location that is easy for families to get to. Be there to answer questions and share information. Encourage families to be involved and let them know that translation is available. If the principal does not speak the language, the interpreter should be a parent, not a school employee. All families, even those for whom English is not a first language, need to know that their children are important to the school and that there is a huge opportunity for involvement and success.

The way to work with families and get them to be engaged with your school is to treat them individually. You will garner support, engagement, and involvement, one family at a time. It might take you a while, but the rewards are worth the effort.

When families and guests visit the school, make sure that the people they need to see are accessible. Often, families will arrive at a school unannounced and the school reacts negatively to this situation. Every time a family member enters a school, it is an opportunity to establish a relationship. Work to make someone available to talk with the family. With so many transient families in our country, every school should have a plan to welcome those families visiting for the first time. A positive first impression will lead to a family deciding to purchase a home in the attendance area of your school. More importantly, they will tell friends and coworkers of their experiences and decision. Often we tend to label families as "hard to reach." It is important that we eliminate this thinking and work to remove whatever barriers exist in forming successful relationships with all families.

15. DOES YOUR SCHOOL PROVIDE TRANSLATION SERVICES FOR FAMILIES WHO DO NOT SPEAK ENGLISH?

Translation is becoming more and more of a challenge for schools. At the high school level, foreign language teachers and native foreign speakers can be given duties as "on call" translators. But that does not go quite far enough. If you are successful in encouraging a non-English-speaking family to come to school, there is a good chance they will be intimidated, uncomfortable, and certainly reluctant. Given this premise, we cannot expect that these special guests to our school can or will ask for translation. Try this: Incorporated into your teacher duties and parent volunteer program, have a greeter at the door who wears a button that says "I speak _____" in the native language. If guests enter your building and do not speak English, they can instantly see that someone speaks their language, and are more likely to feel comfortable, welcome, and willing to engage in a conversation. All of this benefits their children in the long run.

Advertise the ability for the school to translate. Let families know, in their native language, how to get translation, so that if it is not at the ready, it is not a process with which they are unfamiliar. Breaking down the barrier of language and culture goes a long way to forming successful relationships that lead to engaged families and positive school cultures.

16. DOES YOUR SCHOOL MINIMIZE THE USE OF EDUCATIONAL JARGON?

What is most critical in written and spoken communication is the ability for the reader or listener to understand the message. We often get trapped in our own educational language, complete with jargon and mnemonics that only educators understand. It is quite common for a special educator, for example to say, "Based on the situation, we may have to go to an MDR or an FBA before the triennial, but first, let's take a look at the IEP addendum." This type of "eduspeak" becomes very common and often, without realizing it, we begin to speak to families in a language they may not understand.

When communicating with families, use plain, simple language. Sometimes it might be beneficial for parent volunteers to read the letter or correspondence and provide feedback as to its meaning. More often than not, we begin letters with the salutation "Dear Parent/Guardian." This salutation is a bit impersonal, but seemingly necessary to avoid assuming that all adults are parents. A better solution would be to use the salutation "Dear (School) Families." Use of the word family covers every imaginable home situation. Regardless of the relationship to the child or the permanency of the relationship, the adult in a child's life at that time is, in fact, family.

17. WHAT FAMILY EDUCATION PROGRAMS DOES YOUR SCHOOL PROVIDE?

Involving and engaging families in the educational lives of their children requires a commitment to the education of families. In order for all families to have a better understanding of educational programs and practices and to have more meaningful conversations with their children, schools must make the effort to offer programs that assist families in this regard.

To ensure that programs are meaningful to families, schools should survey families and determine their needs and interests. Schools can then offer courses and workshops based on family interest that will improve participation. As a result of this process, Stonewall Jackson High School created the LEAP (Linking Education and Parents) program. Parents and families sign up for workshops and presentations on a variety of academic topics such as algebraic concepts and research paper requirements, guidance-related subjects such as financial aid and post–high school options, and general subjects such as understanding the Internet.

Funding for these types of programs is usually an issue that prevents schools from implementing and offering them. It is important that teachers who work in these programs be paid. There are materials and publicity costs associated as well. Consider that many businesses have already recognized that helping employees be better parents in turn helps them to be better employees. Suggest to local businesses that they help fund these programs and that their employees who are parents can take advantage of them. Look at grant opportunities for additional funding as well. You might be surprised at the financial resources available right in your own community. There is also a great willingness on the part of business and industry to promote positive parenting as well. Capitalize on these avenues to create successful programs for your school.

18. DO STAFF MEMBERS TREAT FAMILIES COURTEOUSLY?

Basic customer service orientation is a component of teacher staff development that seems to be lacking in schools. More often than not, teachers lack exposure to professional development opportunities in the area of family engagement and customer service. Interaction between teachers and families is often limited to brief encounters at annual open house events, guidance conferences, or in situations of confrontation. Schools spend little time working with teachers to create positive and healthy relationships with families and even less time on scheduling staff and professional development opportunities that are open to both teachers and families.

Conferences between educators and families are productive and positive if educators begin the process believing that the conference will be productive and positive. School leaders should assist teachers in creating positive attitudes about working with families and help them to understand that not all interactions are negative. Remind teachers that families care about their children and want the best for their children. Help teachers to describe problems in concrete and objective terms, rather than in an emotional or subjective manner. Use of the word "we" as opposed to "I" or "you" goes a long way in demonstrating a willingness to work together for the success of the child.

Sometimes families do become defensive. Train teachers to seek a commonality on a higher plane that both the parent and teacher can agree upon. Tell teachers that the best thing to do in a situation where they find themselves wrong is to admit it and move on. And, in those rare occasions when parents are belligerent and disrespectful, give teachers the necessary training in ending the conference and suggesting other times to meet. Many of the problems that we deal with on a daily basis can be handled effectively if we place importance on the training and development of teachers in the area of family involvement and communication with all families.

7

ENGAGING FAMILIES

Mission and Governance
Believing that family involvement can produce improved academic success is the first and most important step to improving your school culture. Consider the following system and process enhancements:

1. IN WHAT KINDS OF INITIATIVES DOES YOUR SCHOOL ENGAGE TO PROMOTE FAMILY ENGAGEMENT?

This one question could take your committee hours and hours to answer. This question provides the baseline data necessary to begin an extensive evaluation of existing procedures as well as the development and implementation of new ideas.

Perhaps the best way to facilitate this process is to use a brainstorming technique with the group. On large sheets of blank paper, challenge the group to identify all of the existing practices, policies, procedures, and programs that encourage family engagement with school. The art of brainstorming has a central component in that the entire process is spontaneous and nonjudgmental. Participants should be free to give any example they wish and to see that example written on the sheet of paper. If the group begins to judge each of the answers, the committee will soon get bogged down in details better left for later discussion. More importantly, judging answers at this early juncture in the committee's work will inhibit the future participation of committee members.

A great way to begin the brainstorming activity is to get the group's creative juices flowing with a fun exercise. The leader should pick an common item, such as a rubber band, a pencil, or a paper clip, and inform the group that due to a mistake in the purchasing department, 500,000 of the item has been shipped to the school and cannot be returned. Challenge the group to come up with as many uses for the item as possible in three to five minutes. Teach the cardinal rule of brainstorming: all ideas are good in a nonjudgmental atmosphere. Clarification of ideas can be done at a later time. The group will find this fun and it is a good way to segue into the important brainstorming of family engagement practices at the school. Be sure to include all perspectives of the group. Differences of opinion can be sorted out and clarified at a later time.

2. DOES YOUR SCHOOL HAVE A WRITTEN POLICY OR GOAL REGARDING FAMILY INVOLVEMENT?

Educational leaders accept the notion of high standards and expectations for students and teachers but rarely consider standards and expectations for family engagement with school. Developing a policy is the first step to ensure that any program designed to create strong family partnerships with schools and the engagement of families in the educational lives of children will be a reality and will have attainable and measurable results. When launching a family involvement policy and program in any school, it may be necessary to come to terms with the fact that leadership is shared and that in order to do so, one must subscribe to true collaboration and consensus building for the sake of the relationships that must be built to engage all students in their own learning. The National Coalition for Parent Involvement in Education (NCPIE) policy development guidelines are listed in the appendix. Any school has the potential to create sound engagement programs by following the NCPIE recipe for success.

Most schools and school districts have developed a good system for creating measurable and attainable strategic plans. The appendix contains a planning form that can be used as a way to implement various facets of a family engagement policy and plan. For example, if all families are to receive a copy of the school mission, there are numerous planning questions that need to be asked: (1) Who will be responsible for seeing that this gets accomplished? (2) When will this get accomplished? (3) How much will it cost to accomplish this, and (4) How will we know we have accomplished our goal (objective, strategy)?

3. IS FAMILY ENGAGEMENT INCORPORATED INTO THE MISSION OF YOUR SCHOOL?

Many corporations in America proudly display their company mission, vision, value, and of late, culture statements. Corporate America has learned of the value in immersing all employees and customers in the vision, mission, and culture of the company. Unfortunately, we rarely see this same commitment to vision inside our schools.

Upon entering Stonewall Jackson High School, all visitors immediately come upon a large wall placard that houses the mission statement for the school. Every classroom and office also has the mission statement, in a smaller version, attached where students and guests can see it. The Stonewall Jackson mission statement reads:

> The Stonewall Jackson High School learning community will provide creative and stimulating programs that elevate the achievement of every student to his or her highest potential by establishing high standards and expectations for participation and achievement in a variety of challenging curricular and co-curricular activities. The climate for student learning and staff effectiveness will be maximized by promoting strong family involvement, providing instruction from a global perspective, and emphasizing diversity and acceptance.

The mission of any school must include families. Whether the phrase is family support, family involvement, family partnerships, or family engagement, the important component is that you welcome the involvement of all families in every aspect of the school and its mission to produce high-achieving students. Remember, what gets measured, gets done.

4. ARE FAMILIES AWARE OF THE MISSION AND VISION OF YOUR SCHOOL? HOW HAVE THEY BEEN MADE AWARE?

So often, families have little or no idea of the mission or vision of their child's school. Reflect on these questions: How many times has a parent called and asked that their student be placed in a less rigorous course? How many times has a parent said "No one at that school cares about my child?" How big is your silent majority? When was the last time you took a satisfaction survey of families? What is the rate of failure at your school? How many parents of students who failed came to see you? How often do you compare and contrast your course offerings to your vision and mission of the school? How do you communicate your course information as part of your vision and mission to families?

If corporate America posts their mission statements in every hallway and in every office, then we should do the same. If they spend unbridled energy on sharing the vision and mission of their company with their clients, so too should we spend energy on sharing our goals and dreams for our students with our customers: their families.

5. ARE FAMILY MEMBERS INCLUDED IN STAFF/ PROFESSIONAL DEVELOPMENT PROGRAMS?

Consider staff/professional development programs that invite both families and teachers to participate together. Have them work side by side with such traditional issues as learning styles and instructional methodology. There are many who believe that the best way to find out how a student learns is to ask the student's family. Families will attend in small numbers initially, but as you build your programs and the word gets out of your desire to have families involved, the numbers will grow. Go through the staff or professional development offerings and identify ways to include families in all aspects of educational training and development. Whether it be as complex as Howard Gardner's Multiple Intelligences or something as simple as grading, parents and families welcome the opportunity to learn more about what is happening with their children. This newfound knowledge translates into better relationships in homes, better relationships between teachers and families, better home learning environments, and more support for teachers and their classroom efforts.

6. ARE FAMILIES PART OF THE SCHOOL GOVERNING COUNCIL?

Families and students need to be a formative piece of the governance of any school. Most schools have some sort of council that works to help propel the school forward in the quest for continuous improvement. Make sure that the parents and family members on that council represent all areas from which you draw children, not just a few. It is much easier to get some parents to be involved than it is others. Include family members in group process training to ensure their equitable participation on the committee.

7. HOW ARE FAMILY MEMBERS SELECTED TO BE ON THE SCHOOL GOVERNING COUNCIL?

The most logical way to solicit family involvement in school governing councils is to start with a firm set of bylaws that dictate the process. Most importantly, there should be a process. If the selection of family members is left up to the school leader or other families, it is very likely that the council will not represent the diversity of the school population. As school leaders, we find ourselves embroiled in controversy when there is a perception that the decisions were not made with a process in place.

How the selection process is developed varies from school to school. It is worthwhile to do a geographic or demographic analysis of the attendance area and divide it up, making sure that each of the areas is always represented on the council. If there are differing neighborhoods, then each of them should be represented. Ethnic and economic diversity should also be considered when formulating a plan for family representation on the school governing council. However the process is defined, the most important aspect is that it is an inclusive process.

8. IS EACH DEMOGRAPHIC AREA REPRESENTED ON YOUR SCHOOL COUNCIL?

School leaders must make the effort to find parents and family members who are most likely disengaged or disillusioned with the school and convince them to become an active part of helping the school council guide your school. It will take work and there will be some disappointment when many say "no," but like a persistent salesman, simply shake off the "no" and go on to the next person. Make the effort to identify different neighborhoods and families in order to ensure that each of these areas is represented. Eventually, you will find someone who is willing to take the risk and become involved. Helping families be successful, listening to their ideas, training them to be productive members of the team, and empowering them to help create school improvement plans will have provided them with a positive experience that they, in turn, will share with other parents. That kind of publicity is priceless and is how school cultures are transformed from negative to positive, from dormant to alive, from existing to thriving.

9. DOES YOUR SCHOOL TRAIN FAMILIES TO PARTICIPATE IN SCHOOL GOVERNANCE?

Training families to become thriving and contributing members of your school governance team is perhaps the single most important aspect of family involvement in school governance that will dictate the rate at which you succeed and improve. Consider beginning with basic group dynamics training. Teach all of your members that there are different kinds of involvement and that all need to be respected. Allow different kinds of people to interact with your council, so that unusual behaviors or those who are different from what we know are understood and accepted. Role-play with family members and put them in situations; teach them how to respond.

An important aspect of school governance is consensus. Consensus building is the very best way in which to come to agreement on decisions within your council. Consensus simply means that while individual members may not have come away with everything they thought should be included in a particular proposal, they have listened and compromised and can support the proposal in its final form. Teach your parents how to be involved, verbally and nonverbally, using proven techniques like brainstorming and clustering of ideas. Give everyone a chance to be heard, whether or not they choose to speak. These types of ideas presented in training will ensure long-term, successful group processes.

Availability and Time

Time is the largest barrier educational leaders face when developing, implementing, and sustaining family engagement programs. Breaking down the barrier of time means trying new ideas, reaching out to disengaged families, and breaking old paradigms of traditional thinking about school access.

10. ARE NONSCHOOL HOURS USED FOR FAMILY CONFERENCES WITH STAFF?

Traditionally, school conferences take place either after school or during the school day when school personnel are available. Most families, especially those with parents who have more than one job, either endure great difficulty in attending these meetings or cannot attend at the prescribed time. In some cases, language barriers do not permit the parent to contact the school and indicate they cannot be present at the conference. There are also times when the notification of the conference arrives too late or is in a language that family members cannot read. When this occurs, school personnel get the distinct impression that families do not care about the issues or are apathetic toward their child's education. Nothing could be further from the truth.

Most school leaders have the opportunity to provide flexible staff hours. Perhaps it is not a common practice at your school, but check into your personnel regulations. Often, teachers are contracted to a number of hours, but not necessarily specific start and end times. In cases where unions negotiate contracts, begin to dialogue about flexible schedules or alternative times. The major teacher unions believe that family involvement is vital to the success of every child and should be receptive to working out compromises for teachers to be available to families at alternative or nontraditional times.

Each association provides research-based best practice for members to embrace the concept of family involvement as well as resources for families.[1]

If your school or district deems flexible schedules impossible, try looking into grants and available monies that can pay staff to be at work during evening or weekend times. There is a healthy supply of educational grant opportunities dedicated to family involvement that would be very friendly to a school that wanted to provide services to families at times when school staff are not traditionally at work. Investigate the use of Title I funding as a way to finance these types of extended programs. Consider, too, that businesses are friendly to the idea of their parent-employees meeting about school during nonwork times and may be willing to enter a partnership to fund such arrangements.

Teachers want to meet with parents and most are willing to go the extra mile and stay later than normal or come in on Saturday mornings. As the culture of your school changes and the need to provide financial incentives diminishes, make sure to treat teachers as professionals and never assume they can give of their personal time or that it is the desire of every teacher to do so. As you cultivate and nurture the culture of the school, teacher attitudes and perceptions will change—but it is not an overnight process.

If moving or adjusting the school schedule is an impossibility, provide a family ambassador program that can call families and remind them of conferences and answer any questions that may exist. This concept is similar to the telephone calls that physicians' offices make prior to appointments. A helpful reminder that includes information will be well received by all families.

11. ARE SCHOOL/FAMILY ACTIVITIES HELD IN PLACES OTHER THAN THE SCHOOL (I.E., CLOSER TO CERTAIN COMMUNITIES)?

An important concept to embrace when creating family engagement programs is outreach. Family engagement programs designed by schools must

---

[1] For more information, visit the National Education Association (NEA) website at www.nea.org and the American Federation of Teachers (AFT) website at www.aft.org.

include plans to reach families in places other than the school. Community centers, church recreation rooms and basements, apartment and condominium community rooms, local club or organization meeting rooms, and similar venues should all be factored into a family outreach program. Because of the intimidation and uncertainty among many parents and families about school, there is a better chance that these families will attend events outside of the school in places where they feel more comfortable.

Many school leaders have the experience of planning a meeting or event thought to be important or of interest to the community only to have few people attend. Often, the assumption is that families are apathetic toward the school or particular program. The more likely reasons for this lack of participation lie within those barriers that prevent families from being engaged with their children's school. Barriers of time, culture, transportation, and uncertainty are the more likely reasons that families do not attend school functions. When school leaders reach out to families, especially those who are non-English speakers, important relationships for student success are established.

In many communities, school–church alliances are being formed as a way to provide additional resources to students. School leaders should consider visiting churches on the church members' day of worship. Ask local clergy for a few minutes to talk about welcoming all families to school. They might be more than happy to provide this forum. At the end of the service, many of the ministers and pastors might allow you to stand in the receiving line to greet families. Use these types of opportunities to establish yourself not only as a school leader but a community leader as well. The more recognizable and approachable you are, the more opportunities there are for making strong partnerships with families.

Everyone goes to the mall. About five years ago, Stonewall Jackson entered into a grant program with the mall and the local library system to install a computer lab in a vacant storefront on the main corridor of the mall. The premise of this project was to allow community members who might not have Internet access an opportunity to use computers and the Internet in order to know what the library system offered. On each of the computer screens was the link to Stonewall Jackson and the technology system. Parents and families were taught how to get access to their children's grades and attendance information. Stonewall Jackson students acted as volunteers who manned the computer center and helped citizens navigate the technology. The idea was an instant hit with the community.

Outreach is a significant and important component to successful family engagement programs. School leaders should work with communities to develop as many avenues as possible to reach families in various places in and around the community.

12. DO YOU PROMOTE FAMILY VISITATIONS DURING THE SCHOOL DAY?

This is an area that seems sacred to educators. For some reason, many schools have a rule in place that either forbids the visitation to classrooms by families or severely limits how and when visitation can occur. The origins of this issue may be imbedded in school personnel's basic mistrust of families that has developed over the years. Many educators feel that if a parent wants to observe a classroom, then there must be an agenda against the teacher or the school, rather than considering that a parent simply wants to know what is happening in his or her child's educational life. It is this fundamental change in mind-set that school leaders and teachers need to make in order to establish healthy relationships with all parents.

If family engagement is cultivated correctly, the paradigm of these visitations will change. When school personnel encourage and welcome these visitations, and make the school accessible, the barrier of mistrust that plagues so many schools can begin to crumble. To make school visitations successful and positive, establish a few simple rules. Those rules may include the preservation of instructional time or minimal disruption during testing. Work on this policy with your school governing committee and let everyone have a voice in how the policy can be developed. Many policies require families to give twenty-four hours' notice if they wish to visit a classroom, but some families may not be able to comply with this rule. Further, it is important to treat teachers as professionals and assume that they are prepared to deliver their daily lesson, regardless of who might be observing.

Building positive school cultures implies building trusting relationships. Do not craft school policies about families based on the handful who are difficult or unfair. Create and implement family policies based on the large silent majority who need to be encouraged to be involved and for those whom we know want to be involved for the right reasons. And for those who want to be involved for the wrong reasons, help them to learn and understand the right reasons. Most of the negative relationships between families and schools are built on mistrust. Trusting relationships build positive cultures. Invite them to come to school and see for themselves that the school staff is sincere in its quest to involve families.

Stonewall Jackson High School has one of the largest International Baccalaureate programs in the world. Because of this program and the policy of school choice within the Prince William County School Division, many families are in and out of the school. Often, families ask if they can make an appointment to tour the school. School staff members are glad to accommodate an appointment, but inform the family that an appointment is not necessary. Families are encouraged to come at a time of their choosing to visit the building and see a normal school day for themselves. Inform families that the best way to choose a school for their children is to be in school when it is in session: visit classrooms, the lunchroom, and other areas to get a sense of what a school is about. Selecting a school for children is one of the most important decisions a parent can make. School leaders who welcome visits by families send a powerful message about the culture of the school. During a time when many would like to see public schools replaced with more private options, there is no better way of promoting a school than to allow people to visit and speak to the wonderful teachers and students and see learning in action.

13. DOES YOUR SCHOOL OFFER FAMILIES HELP WITH TRANSPORTATION OR BABY-SITTING FOR SCHEDULED EVENTS?

One of the realities of families who are disengaged with school, especially with those activities that take place at the school, is a lack of available transportation available to many families. A way to combat this issue is to begin to provide bus transportation. Making this type of transportation available and advertising this to families (in native languages) ensures a successful program. Perhaps the first time the buses are sent out, only a handful of families will take advantage of the program. But with time and commitment, the program will be a success and very much appreciated by families for whom transportation is an issue. When the school program is too large to move off the campus and into neighborhoods, provide transportation to those families who need it. This type of program will result in a dramatic increase in participation from families who have never been at your school. There are many schools that are impossible to reach by walking. Consider your school and its access when designing transportation services for families.

For the exact same reason that many fast-food establishments have play areas for children, so should schools offer child-care services during school events. Many schools have child-care programs, PTA/PTSO, community service, and volunteer programs. Use these programs to provide child care for parents who are attending your school event. They are most appreciative of the assistance.

8

COMMUNICATION AND INTERACTION WITH ALL FAMILIES

Communication between homes and schools must be consistent, meaningful, and most importantly, two-way. School leaders should take the initiative to create vehicles to achieve this goal.

1. HOW ARE FAMILIES PROVIDED CONTACT INFORMATION FOR ALL STAFF MEMBERS? IS THE INFORMATION ACCESSIBLE BY ALL FAMILIES?

As children progress through school, the ability for families to communicate with teachers becomes increasingly challenging. Generally speaking, in elementary school, families have one classroom teacher whom they know they can contact with questions or concerns. As children grow older and enter middle school, one teacher becomes a team of teachers; in high school, as many as nine different teachers—with the addition of coaches, club sponsors, alpha or grade-level guidance counselors, and administrators—meaningful communication becomes exponentially more difficult.

Families can best be served with specific contact information for all school employees. For example, it is quite possible that the secretary becomes the first contact when a family calls the school to speak to an administrator. Publishing the names of school secretaries or receptionists is a small but significant step in making communication easier for families. Let families know the names of all staff, especially cafeteria workers, bus drivers, and those nonteaching personnel who are vital to the operation of any school, as well as the names and appropriate contact information for all teaching staff.

Publish this information in more than one language and publicize the fact that it is available. Have multiple copies of contact information in all offices and waiting areas. Publicize this type of contact information at school and athletic events, using the backs of programs, or other types of inserts. Creativity can enhance efforts with ideas such as bookmarks, postcards, magnets, memo pads, and similar items. A consistent effort to disseminate this information results in a clear message being sent to all families that communication is welcome.

Consider the concept of outreach when publicizing contact information. Remember, many parents have never attended a school function or been at the school for any reason. Look within the community for opportunities. The same places that are helpful in hosting outreach meetings can also be used to provide this type of literature. Work with community groups such as the chamber of commerce or Rotary and ask for their help in publicizing contact information for families. Church bulletins are also a wonderful way to provide families with school contact information.

2. DO FAMILIES HAVE APPROPRIATE TELEPHONE NUMBERS, E-MAIL, AND WEBSITE ADDRESSES FOR THE SCHOOL AND ITS FACULTY?

As was stated in chapter 4, technology plays an increasingly important role in establishing positive two-way communication. E-mail addresses should be established for all teachers, who should have access to the Internet via their own computers, and there should be a telephone in every classroom. School websites should be family friendly, allowing for communication from home to school. If it is possible to invest in a telecommunications and Internet system, the ability to enhance two-way communication is improved significantly.

3. WHAT IS THE SCHOOL POLICY FOR TEACHER COMMUNICATION WITH ALL FAMILIES?

Educators pledge at the onset of each school year to improve their efforts in contacting families with positive news and information, but the reality of the job all but prohibits teachers from fitting this goal into their daily rituals, which are becoming more complex each year. Thus, the communication between teachers and families is often limited to negative information about grades, achievement, or behavior. Families often feel they are not informed about their children's progress, or lack of progress, and ask the question "Why didn't you call me?"

To some, it seems odd to have a policy for communication. After all, aren't teachers expected to communicate with families? Even though the very lifeblood of successful schools centers on communication, there can be negative attitudes and confusion about communication. Much like the expectations for family engagement, create a policy for communication so that the "good news" about school can get out to families. Phone calls, postcards, speed notes, good news grams, "atta boys" or "atta girls," and other forms of communication all play a role in building a positive school culture.

Consider providing postcards to teachers so that they can share information with families. Create a drop box for the cards so that teachers can fill them out and drop them in a central location. Office staff or administration should take care of postage and mailing. This idea will start small, but grow quickly in popularity amongst teachers and families.

4. IS THERE A POLICY FOR FAMILY COMMUNICATION WITH TEACHERS?

Educators understand the importance of communication with all families. Unfortunately, the efforts do not always produce the desired outcomes.

Many schools have stringent guidelines about family communication: "You cannot visit the school during the day," "You may not visit classrooms unannounced," "You may not call a teacher during the school day," or "Conferences are only scheduled at certain times"—the list of "don'ts" far outweighs the list of "do's." One of the biggest criticisms that families level against schools is the inability to communicate and get information. These perceptions can be improved with just a few changes in the way families receive help to communicate with schools.

Write and publicize a policy regarding the school's desire to welcome and encourage family communication. Publicize the policies about visitations, telephone calls, conferences, and other forms of communication. Let all families know that communication is not only welcomed but also necessary if the school and families are to work together to help all students learn.

Every employee at a school should have voice mail, similar to employees in the private sector. Voice-mail capability eliminates the problem of "telephone tag" and significantly reduces the chances that a concern will be left without a response.

5. DO ALL TEACHERS COMMUNICATE REGULARLY WITH FAMILIES?

The term *regularly* can mean different things to different people. Some teachers call or write to families on a daily or weekly basis. Some teachers feel that the interim and grade reports sent every four to six weeks is sufficient communication. Take a survey of how often your teachers are communicating with parents by any means, and share that information with staff. Set goals for regular and frequent communication.

As important as sharing this information with teachers is explaining why regular communication is important. A healthy partnership between teachers and families begins with frequent two-way communication. Keep in mind that many teacher preparation programs do not contain a family involvement component in the curriculum. Many teachers do not completely understand the rationale behind communication with families. If teachers have negative experiences with communication, then the degree to which they embrace the concept diminishes.

6. HOW DOES THE SCHOOL ASSIST FAMILIES WITH UNDERSTANDING EDUCATIONAL OBJECTIVES?

The information that schools communicate to families usually has to do with rules, regulations, expectations, forms, fund-raising, and events. The communication of educational objectives is secondary to the above-mentioned information. Families would be well served knowing what the school expects from students and families, what the school deems important in the process of education, the school's position on rigor and challenge within the curriculum, and how the school can assist with educational choices and decisions. Traditional means of communicating course objectives through syllabi, back-to-school nights, and conferences do not go far enough in communicating important educational objectives.

Be sure that all families have access to the school plan. Place copies of it in local libraries and place one on the Internet. Constantly remind families that the school plan, the document that drives the school, is always available for their review and input. Conduct surveys of family interests with regard to educational issues. Families want to know more about course requirements, specific course content (e.g., how can I help my child with algebra?), and critical items such as mandatory testing and graduation requirements.

Stonewall Jackson High School developed the LEAP (Linking Education and Parents) program to begin to address these issues. LEAP is designed to take those items of interest to parents and put them into an instructional format so that parents can not only learn about these issues but be taught how to help their children. Families want to help their children but simply don't know how. If school leaders can find ways to assist those families, then those ideals that we seek for home learning and support for our efforts will come to fruition. Work with your community; find out what their needs are and then work to meet their needs.

There is a business adage that seems appropriate to share. Often, businesses remind sales personnel and employees that while it takes months and months to gain the confidence of customers, it only takes minutes to lose that confidence. School leaders are cautioned that implementing these ideas is important, but the true measure of success will be the degree to which these concepts are sustained and become engrained within the culture of the school.

7. HOW OFTEN ARE GRADE AND ASSIGNMENT INFORMATION MADE AVAILABLE TO FAMILIES?

Interim reports and report cards are the traditional means of communicating student progress to families. Providing crucial academic information to families every four to six weeks is woefully inadequate in ensuring that all children learn at their highest level. Involving and engaging families in the educational lives of their children means creating pathways that provide continuous information about student achievement and experiences in school. The concept of frequent, two-way communication must include not only student achievement but also the communication of curricular goals and mastery of learning objectives to all families so that they may become partners in the education of their children.

It goes without saying that the use of technology can greatly enhance the dissemination of student achievement information on a frequent and regular basis. However, if the necessary technology is not available to schools or families, then procedures and practices can be put into place so that families have more information about not only how their child is doing in school but also what is being taught and how families can support the learning that is taking place in school.

Progress reports, interactive homework assignments that include families, telephone calls, postcards, voice mail, conferences, work folders, progress reports, programs to educate families about curriculum and instructional expectations, and a host of other initiatives go a long way to provide frequent information to families about school. School leaders should work with their school councils or governing bodies to create avenues for this type of information to flow to parents on a regular basis. Consider how the community best receives information and use that information to build a communication program that will help all families be true partners in the education of all students.

8. IS CURRICULUM INFORMATION PROVIDED TO ALL FAMILIES IN AN EASILY UNDERSTOOD, JARGON-FREE FORMAT?

There are inherent challenges in sharing curricular information with families in a manner that can be understood. We do so by creating course syllabi and learning objectives that are written with families in mind. We explain what is to be taught, why it is to be taught, when it is to be taught, and the basic concepts the student needs to know. We replace words like "mastery" with "will know." It is not a question of dumbing down our communication but rather writing documents that can be easily understood by all parents and families.

Above all is the importance of the notion that we must expend time and energy in making this type of information available to families. We must shrug off the idea that families do not care or otherwise do not wish to accept this information. Families believe—just as we do—in the learning capabilities of their children, and they can assist in the education of young people.

9. DOES YOUR SCHOOL COMMUNICATE IN MULTIPLE LANGUAGES?

There is nary a school today that is not multilingual. Our schools tend to be microcosms of our communities and our communities are becoming increasingly diverse. Distributing and disseminating school information in more than one language is necessary to meet the goal of all students learning at high levels. Schools are still unaccustomed to providing information in more than one language and often, because of time and resources, the information is either not translated, or the translated information does not equal the depth, breadth, and quality of the first language communication.

When translating school information, translations should appear in the same form and format as the first language communication. If, for example, a letter is being written, place the second language on the second side of the letter. If more than one translation is necessary, then attach the translations to the first language letter. Most importantly, they should look identical. If the main letter is on letterhead, the translations should be on letterhead. If there is color in the main letter, then there should be color in the translations. Brochures, flyers, booklets, and other types of materials should all be reproduced exactly, regardless of the language in which they are written. With regard to technology, recordings and websites should also have multilanguage capabilities.

There are resources within each community to help with the task of translation. Most businesses and industries have the very same issues as schools with regard to language. More often than not, instructions are being translated into three or four different languages. Contact local businesses and industries and look for ways in which translation resources can be shared. Perhaps foreign language teachers or teachers who are native to other cultures can be paid to assist businesses and businesses in turn will provide funding for translations at local schools. However the arrangement can be configured, knowing the assets within the community and sharing them will undoubtedly benefit the school and families.

10. ARE SCHOOL POLICIES AND REGULATIONS EASILY ACCESSIBLE?

Like most schools, Stonewall Jackson supplies every student with a student agenda. The first forty pages or so constitute the school handbook of information, rules, and regulations. Almost every question parents and families can ask is answered in the student handbook yet school staff found themselves constantly answering rudimentary questions about discipline, attendance, grades, and other school policies. School staff realized that students rarely, if ever, shared the handbook information with their parents and families. As an extension of the LEAP program, staff created the LEAP handbook. It consists of the very same information that appears in the student handbook, but it is especially printed for parents and families. The "frequently asked questions" portion of the booklet is based on regular questions that school staff members receive from families. The booklet is updated each year to reflect the needs and concerns of families and is distributed in two different languages. The handbook is also posted to the school website.

School leaders and governing bodies should take the time to review how this information is communicated to all families and put into place plans that will help everyone connected to the school receive the information they need in a language they can understand.

11. HOW OFTEN DOES YOUR SCHOOL SEND A NEWSLETTER?

Families cannot and will not read, or will stop reading, newsletters that are not interesting or that do not provide them with the information they are looking for.

School leaders should use the newsletter to directly communicate to families about issues that are relevant and are aligned with supporting learning in school. The more that articles and information are important and relevant to families, the more likely the newsletter will be read. Newsletters should be published monthly with special editions for important events, such as back-to-school events or standardized testing information. Newsletters sent out less often than once per month tend to be lengthy and run the risk of not being read and understood by families.

School newsletters should be short and to the point. Not every area can be featured in every newsletter. Edit the newsletter to avoid long-winded articles or information that is really not necessary to publish. Somewhere along the line, school newsletters became a justification of existence for some areas of our school. Keep the newsletter simple, straightforward, and to the point. Put the title page in color. Have running columns and features so people come to expect certain things or, more importantly, know where to look for information. Every month, print the names of administrators and guidance counselors complete with phone numbers and e-mail addresses. Share important contact and communication information with families and place it in the same location every month. Publish a calendar each month, with every event, not just sports or the PTSO meetings, but everything that is scheduled at the school, as well as where and what time it is scheduled. Lastly, place an electronic version of the newsletter on the school website. If possible, send an electronic version to those who have Internet access. Always advertise on your newsletter pertinent information such as the school phone number and website address.

12. DOES YOUR SCHOOL PUBLISH A CALENDAR?

Every month, on paper and the Internet, and in multiple languages, include all meetings and events that are important to all parents and families. Have students create a giant bulletin board-sized calendar in various colors and designs for particular months so that the student body can see it at a glance. Keep both students and families informed of all activities and events at the school and promote them equally.

13. ARE YOUR SECURITY MEASURES WELL PUBLICIZED?

By far, the questions asked most frequently center on the degree of safety in school. There can be no engagement, no learning, no achievement, unless the school is safe and secure. To that end, school leaders must continuously provide safety and security information to the public and invite the public in to inspect their efforts. This is an important issue; if not dealt with properly, it can inhibit the flow of information about academics and other important topics. Parents and families need to know their children are safe.

14. DO YOU PROVIDE A WRITTEN PROFILE OF YOUR SCHOOL TO SHARE WITH STUDENTS, PARENTS, AND GUESTS?

School profiles tend to be limited to those documents that are either internal to the school or district, or are specifically created to be included in college application materials. Making school profile information available to every family is an important aspect of sharing necessary information. Families want to know how students are achieving at your school. It is to the advantage of the school leader to control how this information is publicized and distributed, rather than waiting for local media to relate specific information. Publish test scores, achievement records, SAT scores, and similar measurements. Most importantly, do not print this information in isolation. Show the trends of your school over the past three years. Avoid comparing your school to other schools. Concentrate on promoting your own achievements—don't provide other schools with free publicity.

The profile can also include the names, phone numbers, and e-mail addresses of personnel in administration and guidance, security, sports, and other departments. List the athletics and activities that are available at your school. Provide a brief history of your school. Highlight accolades, awards, and honors that your school has received. Make this the centerpiece of this publication.

A document that is printed on front and back or in a three-fold brochure style is very appropriate for this type of information. If possible, provide color and a few interesting pictures, especially pictures of students engaged with school. Have plenty of copies available and hand one to every guest and family who visits your school. Send copies to the local chamber of commerce, realtors, the office of economic development, the Moose Lodge, the Lions Club, the Rotary, Kiwanis, doctors' offices, hospital waiting rooms, supermarkets, bowling alleys, malls, restaurants, and anywhere else someone might see it. You never know when or where a conversation about your school will take place. Empower your entire community to be able to answer questions and speak positively about your school.

Opportunities for Interaction
The best type of family engagement continues to focus on as many opportunities as possible for families and schools to interact on behalf of all students.

1. DOES YOUR SCHOOL REQUIRE CONFERENCES WITH ALL FAMILIES OF STUDENTS?

School conferences can be a positive force in connecting families with schools. A great deal of research suggests that conferences be held at times that are more conducive for family involvement and should be a requirement for all families, rather than optional or waiting until problems occur. Recent studies point to student-led conferences as a mechanism to involve students in their own learning.

The same barriers to family engagement that have already been discussed are also present when creating avenues for family conferences. A good idea is to create a family ambassador or liaison program. Solicit the help of different parents or family members to work with you to reach out to disenfranchised families. When contacted by another parent and not a school employee, parents and families can often ask questions without fear and are more likely to participate in the program.

The most intimidating situations for families are those conferences that have to do with special education procedures. Special education is a quagmire for families to understand. From their perspective, families are asked to attend meetings with school personnel they do not know and make important educational decisions about their children when they may or may not have all of the information they need and are too intimidated or unable to ask the questions they have.

A family ambassador program can alleviate much of this discomfort. When special education meetings are scheduled, incorporate special education parents into the process. Have families report fifteen minutes prior to the scheduled meeting. There, they will meet with the family ambassador, who also has a child or children in special education. The ambassador can ensure that paperwork was mailed and understood, can explain procedures in the upcoming meeting, and most importantly, can determine what is important to the parent. The ambassador then can lead the parent or family members into the meeting, introduce them to the committee, and share with the committee what (from the families' perspective) needs to be accomplished. This procedure makes special education conferences, or any conference, much more positive and palatable for families, especially those who are intimidated by the school environment.

2. DOES YOUR SCHOOL REQUIRE FAMILY APPROVAL OF STUDENT COURSE SELECTIONS?

When academic problems occur in school, very often the discussion turns to the appropriateness of the child's placement in the course, section, team, level, and so forth. In many cases, the family seems to be unaware of how their child was placed in the specific course or class in question. At the secondary school level, schools require families to sign course selection sheets, but even with signatures on file, families seem to be in the dark with regard to academic course and program selections.

Use the course selection process to help parents and families understand what courses are required and why challenging oneself in school is a better predictor of college success than grade point average. Put a system in place so that every family has input and is consulted with regard to their children's educational plan.

At the elementary level, educate parents as to groupings and instruction, gifted and special education programs, and how decisions are reached in making classroom assignments. Have this information out long before decisions are made and keep it available on a continuous basis.

At the secondary level, it would be advantageous to adapt the "program of study" mentality for every student in your school. Avoid the "shopping cart" approach to course selections and schedules. Invest the time prior to initial enrollment to create a plan, agree to a plan, sign off on that plan, and remain committed to that plan. Changes are bound to occur, but counselors and teachers can contact parents when changes are evident to discuss ramifications and potential solutions.

Common among secondary schools are students who request to drop courses or drop levels of courses when requirements become difficult. Students complain to their families and families often agree to course schedule changes. These changes are often not in the best interests of children, but once families have signed a letter giving their permission, there is little a school can do to reverse the decision. The concern rests with the degree to which families have the necessary information to make an informed and educated decision with regard to program changes for their child.

Stonewall Jackson implemented a program that makes the dropping of courses a process that is designed to educate all parties before any decision is reached with regard to course changes. When a child wants to change his or her program, the student must obtain the official form from his or her guidance counselor, who meets and discusses this potential change with the student and informs the student's family of the student's request for the change. It is the first of several interventions. Next, the student is responsible for getting signatures from his or her teachers, the department chairperson, the program coordinator, the guidance counselor, and the supervising administrator. All of those people have the opportunity to accept the change or reject the change and to make comments as to why they feel the way they do. The last person to sign the form is the parent. The parent makes a decision based on the information provided by a host of school personnel. If there is a conflict of opinions, a meeting is held to discuss the problem. Sometimes, the problem lands on the desk of the principal. Usually, though, parents and families see that there are more reasons to stay with a program than to leave a course. The numbers of course and program changes at Stonewall Jackson have sharply declined. The process also highlights those occasions when a student is truly misplaced in a course and does need a change. Creating a culture for academic achievement must include educating and involving families in course and program decisions.

Expectations for student progress, teacher accountability, and family involvement must be very high.

3. DO FAMILIES HAVE INPUT ON ALL PROGRAM AND POLICY CHANGES AT YOUR SCHOOL?

The school governing council should plan and direct the school in a collaborative manner and seek as many avenues as possible for input from all families. Include the necessary components of language and outreach when designing these systems. Written surveys, telephone surveys, and comment cards are all great ways to solicit opinions and attitudes about school programs. Parent and family ambassadors along with administrators and teachers can place telephone calls to sample homes and solicit opinions, similar to research or political polling. Many telephone voice-mail systems already have automatic survey software built into them to make this objective a bit easier. The use of focus groups in outreach meetings is also an appropriate way to garner the opinions of families about school programs and policies that affect their children. Involving students in the process of soliciting opinions is also very valuable because these policies and programs affect them directly.

4. DOES YOUR SCHOOL MAINTAIN AN ACTIVE PARENT/ TEACHER/STUDENT ORGANIZATION?
5. DOES YOUR SCHOOL ENCOURAGE AN ACTIVE, WELL-DEFINED VOLUNTEER PROGRAM?

PTOs, PTSOs, PTAs, and similar organizations exist in most, if not all, schools. The degree to which membership is solicited from all families seems to be the difference in whether or not the organization is widely successful, or if it is a small clique of parents and families working through their personal agendas. As family engagement programs develop, so do parent organizations and volunteer programs. The key ingredient to success is remembering that time is limited for everyone. If families make the decision to devote time to a school–parent organization or volunteer program, they need to know that their involvement and contributions are significant, which, in turn, means that the organizations themselves need to be significant.

Parent organizations have membership drives at the onset of every school year. Parents and families pay a small amount and are asked to leave contact information if they are interested in helping the organization. More often than not, the vast majority of parents who join the organization and are willing to devote time are never contacted. This sends a negative message to families or a message that suggests their help is not really needed or appreciated. Parent organizations would be best served to find a mechanism to collect information on the strengths and interests of families. If there are parents who have specific skills and interests, those should be noted. When the time comes that those particular skills or interests are needed, phone calls can be made to those families for assistance. Families will feel good about knowing that their particular skill or interest will be of some value to the organization and the organization will have the expertise and enthusiasm of a family assistance.

Volunteer programs in schools need to be conceptualized by the school before assistance is solicited from families. Too often, schools ask for volunteers and either do not have anything for the volunteers to do or limit volunteer work to clerical assistance. School leaders should help in the creation of a family volunteer program that includes not only clerical and building management issues but instructional and mentoring issues as well. Have these positions defined and know how much time is needed so that volunteers can make informed choices. A vision of family volunteers is an excellent starting point for defining and creating a family ambassador program. Families make excellent mentors to other families.

Challenge families to give one day each to the school. If a school has 500 students and had 500 volunteers, a regular school year would see at least two volunteers per day, every day, for the entire school year. With a defined and organized volunteer program, this can easily be a reality.

Outreach to local agencies and businesses is also a vital component of volunteer programs. Many companies release employees to provide mentoring to students, and local agencies can help define and train volunteers for specific tasks.

Several years ago, Stonewall Jackson High School wanted to provide a realistic interview as part of a résumé-writing unit in tenth-grade English class.

With the help of the parent organization, volunteers, and local business partnerships, over 700 sophomores in high school had the opportunity not only to create a professional résumé but also to interview with a member of the business community. The students were provided instant feedback on their strengths and weaknesses, and the business used the opportunity to train employees in human resource development. Parents and volunteers acted as guides, organizers, and event planners. This program replicates itself each and every year and was highlighted by the U.S. Department of Education.

9

CREATING A COMMUNITY SCHOOL

Schools that are organized as community schools can go farther in meeting student needs and building social capital by increasing the opportunities and interactions with community agencies, organizations, and institutions, which can ultimately support the mission of ensuring that all students learn at their highest level.

1. IS YOUR SCHOOL A COMMUNITY SCHOOL?

The following items are attributes of community schools:

- The school is open to everyone—students, families, and the community, before, during, and after the school day.
- The school is oriented toward the community and uses it as a resource. Students not only engage in academics but community problem-solving as well as community service. A before- and after-school learning component allows students to build on their classroom experiences. The entire community supports the mission of the school—to educate all students.

- The school turns to families, residents, and community partners to garner assets. The entire community, and various constituencies within that community, works to promote high educational achievement for all students. Health services are readily available.
- The school lessens the demands placed on teachers. Various community liaisons and partnerships, resources, and materials, as well as extension and off-campus programs, help to lessen the burden placed on teachers in an arena of high standards.
- The school promotes shared decision making among school staff, students, families, and community. The mechanism represents the school governance model discussed earlier and adds the people involved in the community as other resources from which the school can draw information and to help with strategic planning.
- The school has created community and business partners, each of which has a clear understanding of the mission and vision of the school.

2. ARE YOUR SCHOOL FACILITIES AVAILABLE FOR COMMUNITY USE?

Have a policy that allows and encourages community use of your school. Reaching out to the community through building use is a positive form of public relations. Dance groups, music groups, churches, adult sports leagues, classes, business meetings, and similar events can all benefit from a generous community-use policy. The policy will change the school from a component of the community to a community center. Welcome community activities. It will be easier creating a welcoming environment during the school day as well.

There are always groups looking for spaces to hold meetings, events, and sometimes, church services. Many community-based groups are comprised of non-English-speaking families. Reaching out to these types of groups and offering the use of the school promotes a great deal of positive public relations and goodwill, and in turn helps your school become recognized as a place where all are welcome. Community members who use the school will share their positive experiences within the community and the culture of your school will begin to change.

3. WHAT TYPES OF EXTENDED DAY PROGRAMS EXIST AT YOUR SCHOOL?

A significant component to the community education movement is the degree to which school programs are available to students before and after school. Many of the schools being awarded federal grants have extended and redefined the hours and operation of the school so that students can not only have access to remediation programs but also have opportunities for enrichment in the arts, for example. Many elementary schools have child-care programs before and after school that incorporate educational and enrichment issues. Secondary schools should also seriously consider the use of the building before and after school. With so many children being released from school hours before their parent(s) arrive home from work, these after-school programs become essential in helping all children learn. Further, communities and families stand ready to assist in bringing these types of programs to fruition. Families appreciate the extra support and attention their children receive and communities understand that the successful education of its populace is the greatest asset in sustaining cultural literacy and building social capital. These types of programs also help the school meet its goal of developing academic and nonacademic competencies.

4. IS YOUR SCHOOL EQUIPPED TO BECOME A COMMUNITY LEARNING CENTER?

The U.S. Department of Education no longer holds discretionary grant competitions for the 21st Century Community Learning Centers. The program is transitioning to a state-administered program. Each state's department of education has information on grant requirements.

The 21st Century Community Learning Centers program is an important component of the No Child Left Behind Act and has been reauthorized under Title IV, part B. The program provides for expanded academic enrichment for children who attend low-performing schools. In addition to these academically focused programs, programs in youth development activities, drug and violence prevention, technology education, art, music, and recreation are all factors of the program designed to enhance academic achievement.

The processes involved in engaging families and communities with school correlate directly with the desire to change or improve the culture of the school. When developing the process to determine a community learning center, Parson (1999) provides a good framework for organizing the planning, design, funding, operation, staffing, mission, goals, objectives, and overall evaluation of efforts necessary to promote the concept of a community learning center. This concept of community, remember, is closely associated and has a direct cause-and-effect relationship to the engagement of families in the educational lives of their children.

5. DOES YOUR SCHOOL ACT AS A POLLING PLACE ON ELECTION DAY?

Consider calling the local board of elections and offering the school as a polling place. On Election Day, display artwork, pictures, information, and anything else that demonstrates the programs, curriculum, and strengths of the school. This is a great way to get members of the community, who may or may not have children attending school, to learn about the school. Perhaps they are thinking about sending a child to the school, or they will pass on information to someone who is considering the school. With minimal effort, the school profile and the good things happening at school can be distributed to thousands of community members in a single day. It is also wonderful public relations with the board of elections. Consider too, the opportunity for older students to volunteer their time on Election Day and bring to life studies about government and politics.

6. DOES YOUR SCHOOL HAVE A WEBSITE THAT IS CURRENT AND UPDATED?

The vast majority of schools have developed websites. Unfortunately, most schools were unprepared for the explosion of Internet technology, the costs involved in maintaining a website, and the continuous updating and upkeep necessary to make the technology a viable communication tool. Numerous families visit school websites when considering relocation. Community residents make judgments about schools based, in part, on the information that is available to them. The website can be an important tool in not only providing information but marketing your school as well. When people visit the site and the information is out of date, they most likely will not visit again. If they do choose to visit again and the information is still out of date, they certainly will not visit again. Schools have approached this problem either with having staff or students maintain the site, or contract out to a professional webmaster. Websites should be dynamic, or updated automatically upon start up.

Regardless of how you choose to handle this situation, keep the website simple at first, and communicate basic information: the school name, address, contact information (phone and e-mail), current events and information, policies, names and pictures of administrators, mission and vision statements, school plan, information on school governance council, school history and profile, awards and honors, meetings, calendars, activities, directions to the school, and a general information e-mail address so that guests to the website can send questions to you. An electronic version of the monthly newsletter can also be posted to the site. Register a unique and simple domain name for your school site as well. Something that is memorable, short, or unique is more likely to be visited than a site that is a link off of a school district page that has a complicated address.

Once control of the basic information is successful, the website can be expanded to include classroom, team, or department and program information, faculty information, curriculum information, specific classroom websites, homework and grade information, and similar data. Websites should be usable by non-English-speaking guests as well. As with any new initiative, start small, be successful, and then add more. Avoid the use of "under construction." With regard to your home page, visitors should not have to scroll to see all of the information. All of the information should be visible to a visitor after the page completes loading.

Consider links to other community agencies and services as providing a service to visitors. Linking to local and community agencies and other areas of support within the community are helpful to visitors seeking information beyond the school. Make sure that the school is also a link from the local government page and other appropriate community websites. A bulleted list of website component ideas appears in the appendix.

7. ARE YOUR SCHOOL PLANNING AND CURRICULUM DOCUMENTS AVAILABLE TO THE COMMUNITY?

Use the school library, public library branches, and the school or other community websites to have copies of all pertinent planning and curricular documents available to the community. Send copies to the chamber of commerce and the local economic development agency. Make sure that realtors have pertinent school information as well. If you live in an area with a significant concentration of military families, seek ways to send your school plan and contact information to local military establishments. This allows military families the opportunity to make more informed decisions about relocation.

8. HOW MANY DIFFERENT WAYS DOES YOUR SCHOOL PUBLISH TELEPHONE NUMBERS, FAX NUMBERS, E-MAIL ADDRESSES, AND WEBSITE ADDRESSES FOR THE BENEFIT OF THE COMMUNITY?

When promoting your school or specific programs or when communicating important information, promote and communicate the information in as many different formats as is practical. Use the written word, spoken word, and electronics to get your message out as much as possible. For example, when Stonewall Jackson launched the telecommunications program, members of the administration and staff used newsletters, fliers, banners, pencils, buttons, telephone calls, and the local newspapers to get the word out to families. Work on developing the "five different ways" system for the communication of important information from your school.

9. DOES YOUR SCHOOL HAVE A MARKETING PLAN?

Public education has a shrinking number of supporters. If public education is to get out its message of success and if educators are to convince local constituents of the value of public education, then school leaders need a plan to market their schools. Entire books have been written on this subject. Educators must reject the notion that marketing is not part of their job and must be prepared to confront negative attitudes about marketing in education. The very idea that educators have customers can be a difficult concept to implement. Think of customers in two areas: internal customers (students, teachers, and staff) and external customers (families and communities). Train your staff in these ideas and understand the needs of the various types of customers and what the school can do to meet those needs.

As important as customer service is, so is the idea of school image. There is a great chasm between reality and perception. What communities and families think and feel about a school creates a perception of image. When perceptions are negative, it can take schools years to erase this image; sometimes, they are never successful in doing so. Carroll and Carroll (1994) provide a list that can elevate or destroy a school image.

- Newspaper articles
- Any publications distributed from the school
- Radio and TV reports
- Condition of the physical plant, the grounds, bulletin boards, offices, classrooms, and cafeterias
- Curriculum design
- Standardized and state-mandated test scores, especially SAT scores
- Colleges where seniors are accepted
- Drop-out rate
- Teen pregnancy rate
- Drug and alcohol use
- Athletic program
- Special facilities and equipment (swimming pool, computer hardware and software)
- School–business partnerships
- Student and staff volunteerism in the community
- Teaching and administrative staff outreach, service to the community

When we understand the importance of building community schools, the idea of marketing is essential in the successful development of the collaborative ideals that will help all students.

10. HOW MANY AND WHAT KINDS OF EVENTS ARE HELD EACH YEAR THAT INVOLVE FAMILIES AND COMMUNITY MEMBERS?

The best way to promote and develop a positive school culture is to welcome family and community guests as often as possible. Use business and community partners to create programs that involve local businesses and community members. Activities that involve the community do not have to always be in the evening or center on a special program. The more that the community can be involved and aware, the more likely there will be success in shaping a positive school culture.

Contact the local realtors' board and get the names of every realtor in your general area. Invite them to a breakfast meeting at your school. Provide them with information about your school, its students, faculty, and programs. Educate them as to your programs and successes. Give them materials that they can use with potential home buyers. At the conclusion of the breakfast meeting, give them a tour of your building, especially if there is a negative perception of your school. Do not underestimate the power of realtors to promote your school. They will be grateful for the breakfast and information and they will use it. Breakfast is suggested because those realtors who sit in model homes go to work at 11:00 A.M. or noon, and house hunting with clients does not usually start at 8:00 or 9:00 A.M.

If you are in an area that has a great deal of home construction, develop relationships with those who are selling homes. Provide them with school materials, especially test scores and registration information. Realtors are always asked about schools; when school leaders provide the information, schools can control the information that is being disseminated into the community.

11. HAVE YOU MAPPED THE ASSETS AVAILABLE IN YOUR COMMUNITY?

Mapping community assets can help families orient themselves to the school and community if they are new, answer questions for those who are already connected to the school, and provide important information when transforming a school to a community school. There are a number of different processes available to educational leaders in getting this task done. Asset mapping takes time, patience, and resources; requires the help of parents, students, staff, and community members; and needs focused leadership from school administrators. For resources for community asset mapping, see the appendix.

The Anaheim Union Free High School District parent involvement coordinator, Kim Bauerle, shares a step-by-step process used in Anaheim to help map resources.

First and foremost, the school should put together a focus team. The team should include an administrator, teachers, students, community representatives, business liaisons, representatives from county or city government, and other members pertinent to the school and community. The group should be supplied with three-foot by five-foot enlarged attendance area maps, laminated and framed onto corkboard. Color-coded pushpins and rounded color-coded tags should be available. The team should then undertake a process to define the assets that are important to the school, students, parents, and community. This is the most engaging, tedious, and time-consuming portion of the process. The group should be sure to include parks, health clinics, hospitals, skate parks, businesses, organizations, language-friendly businesses and services, and other categories of assets as defined by the group. The team should then divide the school attendance area and canvass the segments, recording all of the community assets available. The team can assign a color to each asset category and construct a small write-up about each of the assets. A database can also be created to create the ability to pull up like or similar assets within the community. All of this information can be put onto the large attendance map with the color-coded pins, and the information can be cataloged and disseminated to all members of the school community.

12. DOES YOUR SCHOOL HAVE AN ORGANIZED PUBLIC RELATIONS PROGRAM?

Even though we understand the importance of public relations, this topic almost always takes a backseat to the other issues presented to us in school leadership. Generally speaking, this is one of the weakest areas for education. As a principal or school leader, you should take charge of public relations and develop a plan to improve or increase your exposure within the community.

Usually, newspapers cover stories that are of a "breaking news" variety. When Stonewall Jackson launched its telecommunications program, newspaper and other media reporters were uninterested or reluctant to run a story about the innovative technology. Some of the reporters indicated that they would "try" but none of the articles ever appeared in print or on television or radio. The leadership at Stonewall Jackson then took it upon themselves to try one more innovative approach. An article was written as if school employees had been interviewed by reporters, when in all actuality, no interviews took place. A copy of this "breaking news story" was sent to each of the local newspapers, television stations, and radio stations. The article appeared on the front page of two newspapers and was a lead story on the local news radio station.

One of the weakest organizational structures in our schools is that of managing good news. There are so many positive things that happen on a daily and weekly basis that we could fill newspapers with just our "good news." Create a plan to have that information funneled to one central source and then get it out to the local media. Do not rely on individual teachers or sponsors to do it, because they are busy and they just will not get to it. Create standard news release templates (double spaced, contact person, and phone number) and fax the information out almost continuously. If only 10 percent of what is sent actually gets published, it's 10 percent more than would have been published with no effort at all. Stonewall Jackson has enjoyed dozens and dozens of positive articles over the years and this commitment to public relations has definitely helped shape a positive school culture.

Washington Post education feature writer Jay Matthews is the creator of the Challenge Index and was the impetus for the *Newsweek* "Top 100" schools list. Several years ago, Jay became interested in International Baccalaureate (IB) and Advanced Placement (AP) programs. Stonewall Jackson formed a relationship with Jay and provides him a great deal of educational information about the school. As a result, Jay keeps close tabs on the progress of Stonewall Jackson and reports it in a very favorable light to the readers of the *Washington Post*. Jay Matthews has been invited to be a guest speaker at Stonewall Jackson as well. Wherever your school is located, get to know those reporters and media personnel who cover education. Get on a first-name basis with reporters and give them a quick call when something is interesting. Reporters are always looking for a story. For every ten stories you pitch to the media, one might just get published or featured on the local news. Do that every month and you have eight to ten positive features about your school per year.

A telephone call from the media should never go unanswered. The phrases "unavailable for comment," "did not return our phone call," or "was not available by press time" are detrimental phrases to anyone trying to establish a positive relationship with families and communities. Even if you have no comment or cannot comment, return the call and let the reporter know. There is an old saying, "Do not get into an argument with someone who buys his ink by the barrel." It is impossible to control the media, what they choose to report, and how they choose to report it. Take a positive approach and manage and covet the relationship you have with the local media. By the way, there is no such thing as "off the record"! A former associate superintendent once gave a wonderful piece of advice to me when dealing with the media: "The more you say, the more you have to defend." Words to live by.

13. HOW MANY ESTABLISHED BUSINESS AND COMMUNITY PARTNERSHIPS IS YOUR SCHOOL INVOLVED IN?

When reaching out to your community, inviting partnerships with the local business community can pay huge dividends. Already emphasized earlier in this book is the need for the partnership to have a purpose and vision mutually established by the school and its partner. As important as having a vision and plan for family partnerships, so is the need for community and business partnerships. The National Association for Partners in Education offers several excellent references to educators to ensure a smooth planning and development process with regard to business and community partnerships.[1]

---

[1] Visit the National Association of Partners in Education at www.nape.org.

10

ENGAGING FAMILIES WITH STUDENTS

There exists a direct relationship between the engagement of families and the engagement of students. Family engagement acts as a catalyst to help students remain engaged with their own education.

1. HOW OFTEN DO YOU PROVIDE FAMILIES INFORMATION ABOUT THEIR CHILDREN'S ACADEMIC PROGRESS?

Families' expectations of their children almost always manifest themselves into expectations for school achievement, primarily, grade expectations. These families want their children be successful; to meet their dreams, goals, and desires; and often, to do better or go farther in life than they did. Family expectations range from minimally passing classes to children demonstrating their personal best. Families interact in a number of different areas that can be categorized as supporting a student's motivation to be engaged with school.

Family discussions with their children about education and their specific discussions about grades act as motivators to students. In a general sense, students seem to appreciate the discussions and expect their parents to have certain standards for academic achievement and school involvement and performance. Specific conversations about grades usually include praise for good school achievement and encouragement to do even better, which students see as motivating. In order for familial motivation to be a positive force in the life of their children, and in order for that positive force to help their children be motivated to be engaged with school, there exists a balance between praise for achievement, discussion of grades and grade goals, and an expectation that the student understands what is necessary to be successful in school. This balanced combination of support and interaction provides the motivation for engagement.

Student and family interaction about grades or problems can best be characterized by conversations that parents have with their children relative to improving their academic situation. Parents question their child's classes and teachers, as well as homework, when trying to determine the source of the problem. Families also direct their children to get assistance from either their teacher or the school's tutoring program. The most common response to academic problems in school is to either praise the attainment of positive achievement or to discipline the child, in the form of grounding or a hiatus from activities until the grade returns to an acceptable level.

Although all of these research outcomes are important to the overall development of students and positive culture of schools, none of it is possible if basic information about student achievement and progress is not communicated in regular intervals. Traditionally, schools have limited this reporting to interim or report cards. This level of communication is considered minimal by today's standards and not conducive to the engagement of families and students. Schools must find ways to constantly communicate the progress of children to all families. We cannot expect students to be engaged with their own learning when families can only discuss relevant school issues every four to six weeks.

Technology is certainly the most logical answer with regard to the improvement of information flow from school to home about academic achievement. However, weekly folders, reports, telephone calls, and other methods can also be important ways to share pertinent information.

2. HOW DO YOU PROVIDE COCURRICULAR AND ATHLETIC ACTIVITIES INFORMATION TO ALL FAMILIES?

More time in extracurricular activities and less time in jobs and television viewing were associated with higher test scores and class grades (Cooper,

Lindsay, and Nye 2000). Unfortunately, a large number of students do not participate in cocurricular or athletic programs, thus feeding the separation between families and schools. Educating families with regard to the importance of noninstructional activities is an avenue to help engage students and families.

Schools leaders have an academic focus and spend much of their time sharing this type of information with families. While not suggesting that leaders stray from this premise, consideration of sharing information about noninstructional programs with families can help families to understand the programs and the importance of involvement, and can act as a catalyst for families to encourage their children to participate.

Consider a series of postcards. With a digital camera, take pictures of different clubs, programs, teams, and organizations that make up your school. Include before- and after-school programs as well. These pictures can then be created as a postcard relatively inexpensively. Once the postcards are completed, mail them to families with a brief description of the activity and where more information can be obtained. This idea creates discussion among families about school programs. In large schools, students are often unaware of the depth of noninstructional offerings.

Take an inventory of the noninstructional programs in your school. Once complete, seek families who have expertise in particular areas. Perhaps there are family members with computer knowledge who can enhance the computer club, or a parent who enjoys chess and can help sponsor the chess club. Advertise the need for literacy volunteers to participate in after-school or evening programs.

Lastly, understand the importance of marketing and public relations for your school. Develop a yearly magazine or document that can show in pictures and words the accomplishments of your school and the numerous ways in which families and students can involve themselves in programs that are cocurricular in nature.

3. HOW DO YOU PROMOTE HIGH INTEREST IN YOUR SCHOOL BY ALL FAMILIES?

Consider for a moment the activities that draw families into your school: concerts, back-to-school night, games, fairs, meetings, awards programs, commencement ceremonies, and similar events. Now consider the percentage of your total family population that is engaged with your school as a result of these activities. If your school is like most, all of these events combined still do not produce platforms from which a majority of families can be engaged with your school. More often than not, only parents of those students who are involved in a particular activity attend the activity. School leaders have lamented for years a decline in meeting attendance and membership in parent–teacher organizations.

The perception and interest in our schools is maintained in the informal social and community circles that surround the school. On soccer fields, at deli counters, cocktail parties, bus stops, churches, and other places frequented by families, discussions about problems and concerns with school are very common, especially when there is controversy. Families are quick to incorporate the words *that school* into their diatribe of complaints. ("Do you know what *that school* did?" "Don't bother trying to reason with the principal at *that school!*" "I cannot believe *that school* and their latest crazy ideas!") This type of language by families associated with the school suggests no personal investment on the part of those who use these phrases. Even though they may have children who attend, they are not invested in the mission of the school and can be unsupportive of the efforts of the school. These types of attitudes are cancerous, especially when the information is shared with those who are not connected with the school, which is the majority of members in the community. Families get information from three sources: their children, teachers, and other families. School leaders should concentrate on engaging and educating both internal and external customers so that information flow is fluid and correct.

The philosophy of language to which school leaders should aspire is not the words *that school*, but the words *our school* or *my school*. This concept involves a change in attitude, mind-set, and a fundamental shift in the culture of a school. In order to bring about this necessary language of inclusion and engagement, work needs to be done to construct an operating framework from which information flows freely to and from the school. The first and most critical step, and the most difficult and time-consuming step, is to create an educated populace within your building and then to enlist the support of a core team of people outside of your building. One way of looking at the multidimensional properties of this task is to consider a program of ambassadors, much like governments use ambassadors throughout the world.

Teachers as Ambassadors

The best ambassadors (and the best destroyers) of school reputations are the faculty and staff who work in the building. Maintaining open lines of communication and meeting the needs of these internal customers help to provide a basis from which staff can act as positive emissaries throughout the community. Families and community members are cognizant of the fact that those who work within the school have the best and most accurate information about the school. The community will listen intently to what teachers and staff say, and believe much of what they hear at face value, because of the credibility of the source. The best way to promote high interest in your school is to ensure that the faculty is well informed of the programs and opportunities available at the school and can speak to these in any public forum.

An important and often overlooked step in building a positive school culture and promoting family and community engagement is the role that a school's staff can and must play. School leaders need to build a working environment that is conducive to professionalism and one in which teachers and staff are treated professionally and in which all staff are held to the same consistent standards. In a recent workshop conducted by the Family Friendly Schools organization, teachers were asked to answer the following open-ended question: "If there is one thing that I dislike about my school, it is . . . " What surprised workshop leaders was the overwhelming response of teachers: the biggest frustration was not administration, working conditions, apathetic students, or difficult parents. The biggest concern was centered on professional colleagues—other teachers who did not perform in their jobs at the expected level with no obvious consequence. This one issue causes divisiveness and poor morale, and clouds teachers' perceptions of their own schools. Unfortunately, allowed to go unchecked, this attitude will permeate the community because teachers vent their frustrations within the community. A school cannot be productive, nor will families and communities wish to be engaged with a school, where the employees are disgruntled.

The ability for school leaders to provide healthy working climates for teachers and staff is directly related to the degree of success in using teachers as ambassadors of the school. There will always exist a small portion of any workforce that is disgruntled; however, those outside of the school will be quick to learn that the majority of teachers speak intelligently and positively about the school, which will create high interest among families and community.

Students as Ambassadors

The people who are affected most by school policies, procedures, and practices are the students themselves. Families garner the largest amount of information and develop perceptions about school based on what children report. Most children, as was demonstrated at the very onset of this book, say little about their school experiences. During those rare times that students do speak about school, their families listen intently and form opinions and perceptions about their children's school.

The more school leaders can do to create student-centered environments within schools, the more likely that students will take stock in their education. Students should have a voice in all aspects of school governance. At Stonewall Jackson, a program entitled the Student Activities Leadership Council (SALC) was developed to replace the traditional student government association. This organization is attached to a credit-bearing class in leadership. The class is comprised of student leaders from each of the classes as well as the SALC leadership. The remaining slots are open to any student who wishes to participate. A panel of students and teachers interviews students if they are interested in being in the class. The interview process ensures that representation from all facets of the student body is housed within the organization. When an issue is discussed, the athletes, skateboarders, "Goths," and other types of students all participate in developing recommendations to the site governance council. Six of the seats on the school governance council are reserved for students. Four of those six are for officers and the remaining two are at-large seats. The students who fill those positions are at the complete discretion of the students.

This kind of trust and encouragement leads to a more positive school environment. The administration has stepped away from many day-to-day issues and allowed the SALC to develop and implement policies and police the student body. When there is a compliance issue, it is the SALC and not the administration that imposes sanctions. This type of student-centered focus speaks volumes to all students about our trust in them to be able to think and act in a rational and independent manner. It stands to reason that when developing programs, policies, procedures, and practices in a school, those that they most affect—students—should have a significant responsibility in helping to shape the culture.

Students rarely speak about their academic experiences in school. More often than not, they relate information about lunch lines, tardy policies, safety issues, or other noninstructional types of information. It is possible that families are creating perceptions of their children's schools not on their academic prowess, but on the length of the lunch lines and whether or not students feel safe in their schools. Addressing these types of issues allows for all students to be ambassadors for their school.

The best people to speak about school experiences are students. Many years ago, Stonewall Jackson began a program of January meetings with eighth-grade students to help them prepare for high school. The principal, director of guidance, and certain program directors would visit all feeder middle schools and discuss various aspects of the school. The audiences were polite, but there was a sense that the information being shared with the incoming freshmen was not the information they wanted to most know about. A few years ago, the format of these meetings was changed and present high school students shared the majority of information with incoming freshmen. The adults were still present and still addressed the students, but the focus of the program was for students in high school to help eighth-grade students feel better about their transition to Stonewall Jackson. Questions went from few to hundreds of hands. The eyes of the eighth-grade audience came alive and they listened intently as high school students shared their perspective of a school they were very proud of. Most inspiring was the challenge that is laid before the eighth-grade audience. High school seniors insist that incoming freshman carry on the proud tradition of the school by being the best they can be, supporting their school, and becoming involved. Even though adults had said the same thing for years, there was magic when students said it to students.

The phenomenon that occurred as a result of this shift in presentation was inspiring. It became obvious that eighth-grade students were going home and *sharing* information they had learned from their meeting with real, live high school students. Participation in follow-up meetings and breakfasts for families increased threefold. The percentage of students choosing to attend the high school orientation program increased by 600 percent! If there was ever any doubt about the power of student-to-student communication, it was erased during the first encounter between eighth-grade and high school students. The student ambassador program was born.

Families as Ambassadors

The premise of students finding information credible if delivered by other students holds true for families as well. At the onset of the new administration taking charge of Stonewall Jackson in 1995, the reputation of the school was negative. An investigation of how this information was being communicated and transmitted showed discussions between families accounted for the largest segment of information flow. This was especially true of military families, of which there is a high population in the Washington, D.C., area. Families being transferred relied on information from military families already stationed in the area to make decisions about house purchase and school attendance. Feeding this information flow were realtors who officially are to remain noncommittal in discussing schools, but would subtly direct clients to areas they perceived to be better.

Establishing a family ambassador program promotes interest in your school and is a vehicle to disseminate positive and factual information. As part of an ever-evolving program, Stonewall Jackson finds and trains families who agree to make themselves available to new families. This approach allows moms to talk to moms, dads to talk to dads, and maybe most importantly, students to talk to students.

With these efforts to create high interest in the school by sharing factual information, the reputation of Stonewall Jackson High School has changed from negative to positive. More and more families are choosing to locate or relocate within the Stonewall Jackson attendance area because not only do they get factual information from reliable sources but also once involved in the school, their experiences match what they heard.

4. HOW DO YOU ENCOURAGE FAMILY INVOLVEMENT WITH CREATING ENHANCED HOME LEARNING ENVIRONMENTS AND ACTIVITIES?

Research has clearly shown that families who provide positive home learning environments help students to achieve at higher levels in school. Teachers often cite home learning as a significant component of a student's academic success. These ideas, coupled with the notion that a parent is a child's first and best teacher, establish the promotion of positive home learning environments as one of the most significant aspects of family engagement in education. Families want to help their children, but often barriers get in the way of their best intentions. School leaders can assist by giving parents and families the information necessary to not only understand the role of home learning but to make them active participants in their children's home learning.

Communicate the Attributes of a Good Home Learning Environment

We have all heard for years that students need a quiet, well-lit space in which to do their home learning. How often, though, do we share and reinforce this concept with families? As our society changes and the lives of families become more complicated, we must help families help their children. We need to remind families that they should help their children establish routines that enhance productivity at home. The access to different types of media should be limited. Listening to music or having the television on is not the best way for any child to complete assignments. However, there are more than just environmental issues to involving families in healthy home learning experiences.

Explaining Work to Families

As is done with Stonewall Jackson's telecommunication and Internet system, communication about assignments is shared with parents and families on a regular basis. Families need assistance in understanding the details of homework and how to recognize whether or not their children have completed assignments successfully. Simply put, we can help families help teachers check for understanding. Give families the premise upon which the assignment is built, what the assignment should look like, how it should be completed, and an important aspect often left out, how long it should take the child to complete the assignment. As always, teachers should welcome feedback from families about the home learning experience to enhance the reinforcement that occurs within the classroom.

How Families Can Enhance Learning

Television is often painted as an evil and, in many cases, the reliance on television in our society is indeed alarming. However, with the advent of cable and satellite television, numerous educational stations are available to a large majority of families. Teachers can inform families of programs on television that will enhance the lesson or unit being studied in school. Teachers can also suggest trips to museums, galleries, farms, and countless other resources, perhaps right within the community's borders, that will provide an experiential component to the student's learning. Not all parents will act upon these suggestions and, unfortunately, it is this idea that stops us from this kind of activity. Focus not on those who might not assist their children, but on the majority who want to see their children succeed and are willing to support the school with direction, suggestion, and guidance.

Interactive Education

There is a rather tongue-in-cheek notion at many schools that suggests that when the copy machine is out of order, the process of teaching and learning comes to a grinding halt. While this may be an exaggeration, bulging class sizes and shrinking budgets force teachers to rely on creating assignments that can be mass-produced. If teachers were to create homework and lessons that included family participation, the home learning then takes on a new dimension and helps families to be engaged with their children's learning in a different way. Many schools are giving teachers the professional development time to create these types of interactive lessons and curriculum modifications based on the premise that experiential learning and relevancy in learning helps to make instruction come alive.

5. HOW DOES YOUR SCHOOL PROMOTE COMMUNITY SERVICE ACTIVITIES?

The essence of community service is becoming an increasingly popular component of school curriculum. Understanding one's role in a community is, in a sense, the reason for the democratic ideals of public education in the United States. To take one's rightful place within the community and to enhance the republic are the cornerstones set by the earliest common schools.

Community service should be promoted within every school. Students and their families should have opportunities to provide volunteer services throughout the community. If any school leader went into the community and asked if there were opportunities for volunteers to assist, certainly they would be inundated with requests. Parks, hospitals, retirement homes, homeless shelters, and other community agencies are always looking for assistance. Community service can and should be family oriented. Engaging students in the community helps students gain the necessary perspectives for success in life after high school.

It is comforting to know that community service components in school curriculum are on the sharp increase. Programs such as the International Baccalaureate and the Advanced Placement programs now have a community-centered component attached to them. Giving back to one's community is one of the most powerful learning experiences that can take place.

Several years ago, Stonewall Jackson staff became involved in Relay for Life, sponsored by the American Cancer Society. In the first year or two, the Stonewall team consisted of mostly students, with a few teachers who were involved in different aspects of the organizations in which the participating students were involved. Over the years, that small core group of students has blossomed into a large group of teachers, students, and families. Tents are erected, sleeping bags are arranged, and food is delivered by the carload. The teams sing, dance, and support each other during the wee hours of the walk. It was most gratifying this past spring, after a popular parent succumbed to cancer, to see the throng of people represent the school and support the family. Arms locked, the Stonewall team filled the entire width of the track and was several rows deep. Each wore a memento representing the spirit of the fallen parent. Strangers, young and old, came together for a tremendous cause with a unified need. It was a day of absolute pride for the school and none of it took place inside of a classroom.

Whatever or however a school chooses to promote community service, it should be done regularly and throughout every grade level. One is never to young to learn the lesson about the power of giving back.

6. HOW ARE YOUR IMPORTANT EVENTS PROMOTED TO FAMILIES AND THE LARGER COMMUNITY?

Every school has events. If a school has an event, then there must be some importance or relevance attached to the event. Schools commonly fall into the trap of publicizing events only to parents or, in the cases of music concerts, just to the parents of those students performing. Every event hosted by your school is an opportunity to educate and engage parents and community. Using the marketing and public relations information discussed earlier, be sure to publicize every event and take any opportunity to showcase your school. Use free services such as community bulletin boards, church newsletters, local television and radio stations, and other venues to publicize. Send invitations and offer shuttle transportation to retirement centers and local hospitals. Encourage working parents to post flyers and publicize school events. Send invitations to local businesses and ask for their support in publicizing.

All of these ideas take organization, planning, and commitment. When new parents arrive at a school event and see large numbers of people, it leaves a lasting impression as to the degree of involvement between the school and its community.

A COMMITMENT
TO FAMILIES

The involvement of families in the lives of their children remains a strong component to student engagement in school and school-related activities. Families who are involved and engaged with their children and their children's schools can provide their children motivation to do well and achieve to their highest level. Family expectations alone can be a driving force in student engagement. Schools can help families understand standards and expectations as a method of improving student achievement.

A large number of students have strong feelings about their family and their family's involvement with school. For example, chapter 2 discussed that even though students were not overly enthusiastic about their parents' ability to access grade and attendance information with technology, they welcomed their parents' review either to celebrate their successes or to openly discuss problems in school. This interaction between students and their families is important in determining the engagement level of students, which ultimately leads to achievement. If parents use the information to praise their child or help their child, the interaction is welcome. However, if the information was used to belittle their child, demean their child, or punish their child, the information then becomes a deterrent to school engagement.

Whether viewing this phenomenon positively or negatively, one cannot discount the important relationship between children and their parents.

Once again, schools can assist parents in how to work with their child and their child's teacher to use the information in a positive fashion. It certainly could be detrimental to all involved if information is provided with no direction, information, assistance, or parameters for use. When school leaders make the important decision to involve and engage families, they must make a full commitment to assisting families in navigating the world we know as school.

Families who maintain a positive attitude about their children's schools help their children be more engaged and successful. Research has clearly demonstrated that one of the barriers to family involvement is uncertainty about school in general. This uncertainty can take many shapes and forms and is easily transfixed upon students. Students in one study (Constantino 2002) were cognizant of the school's efforts to promote family involvement and, in those cases where students report no real encouragement for engagement from the school, they did report that the positive relationship between the school and their family helped promote more positive parent–child communication.

Students often find that their parents' encouragement and goals for the future assist them in focusing on their own school engagement. Parents who share their dreams, goals, and desires with their children and who continuously reaffirm the importance of education are often a prime force in the engagement of many students. Unfortunately, the parents who choose to compare their children to other children or who tend to fixate on certain aspects of school often provide a clear deterrent to their child's engagement with school.

The need for schools to promote family involvement and engagement can positively affect the attitude and perceptions of families and, ultimately, of students. It is clear that when families have a generally positive view of the school, they share that positive view with their children; subsequently, the children hold a positive view of school as well. This positive attitude promotes discussion between families and students, as well as families and friends.

To further enhance the positive perception and attitude of families and students, teachers must be made to understand that they have a pivotal role as the representatives of the school. Students in numerous studies are fairly consistent in stating that engaged, involved, and caring teachers are prime reasons to be engaged and stay engaged with school. Other school programs, clubs, and activities were not viewed as important. It would serve school principals well to reinforce clear expectations for student engagement with teachers and to provide them with information and professional development with regard to family involvement and student engagement. Students look to their teachers for guidance, learning, support, and assistance. Teachers can be effective and important ambassadors to families and community, and are a driving force in the school's ability to promote family engagement as well as the engagement of individual students.

The style of parenting displayed by families can be enhanced and improved with efforts from the school. Schools can enhance the flow of positive communication between families and students by providing them with information about classes, assignments, grades, activities, and other school-related topics. Most parents discuss these topics with their children and children generally appreciate knowing that their parents care enough to discuss issues, concerns, ideas, and school happenings. As these efforts become immersed in the culture of the school, and the school acts as a catalyst for positive change, more and more parents and families will become involved in the processes.

Establishing effective two-way communication and family involvement to promote the academic success of students is only a portion of the equation. Understanding the power of peers and the in-depth interaction that occurs between individual students and their friends is also necessary to support the engagement of students. High schools with over 1,000 students, for example, could very well be destined to remain nameless and faceless emporiums where students mimic the art of learning but are in a slow decent toward disengagement from education. Outside influences, such as friends, families, jobs, and church, all have an impact on student performance regardless of their age, race, or socioeconomic status. Students in the study cited earlier (Constantino 2002) clearly identified the interaction of friends and nonfamily adults when making decisions about courses and the degree to which they would be involved in school. By positively connecting with and encouraging all families to be engaged, students who rely on the families of friends for information also get the same important messages about school engagement.

Students rely on their families for help, guidance, and assistance. We as school educators cannot hide behind the teaching of responsibility to students as reasons to ignore our role in promoting the involvement and engagement of families in the educational lives of their children. Now more than ever, families need assistance. They need to know how their children are progressing through school and what they can do to support their children's ultimate achievements. Rarely does a parent not want a better life for his or her child. Families sense a real commitment from schools to involve them so they may help their children. Whether they were supportive or unsupportive of the school, interactions with families have a common strand—the success of the child. All those in school leadership positions must continue seeking successful avenues for family involvement, and to also share experiences and ideas with colleagues to promote this often overlooked component to school reform and student success.

Families who feel connected to their children's schools also feel more connected to their children. Having a positive connection with their children's school helps families to support not only a relationship with that school but also relationships with their own children. Countless parents have discussed with me their ability to have conversations about school because of our efforts to share information about their children in a trusting and continuous manner. Families begin to connect with the school, feeling welcome upon entering the building and knowing that, whatever their concern, someone will help them. This attitude that families garner from schools that promote family engagement is an essential component in building a positive school culture that not only permeates the building but the community as well. More schools need to adopt these ideas and implement programs that will bring families, students, and their friends closer together in support of academic success for all.

THE DISCOVERY OF PROOF

The tragedy of September 11, 2001, will be with us forever. It was on that day that tangible proof emerged and demonstrated that the efforts to unite Stonewall Jackson High School and its surrounding community of families over the past eight years were beginning to become part of our school culture.

Hundreds of students at Stonewall Jackson High School have parents who are in the military and who work at the Pentagon in Washington, D.C.

At the very moment of the Pentagon attack, the school crisis plan was put into motion with the knowledge that when students heard of the disaster they would become frantic with worry for their parents and family members. The school auditorium was set up as a place for distraught students to stay while information about the attack became available. The entire counseling staff was on hand to deal with the almost 300 students who appeared once announcements of the problem had been made. Understanding that parents would instinctively want to be with their children at this time of national tragedy, a plan was developed and put into place for what would undoubtedly be an onslaught of parents heading toward the school.

After ensuring the plan was in place, and making sure that staff members who had spouses at the Pentagon were cared for, I took up a position outside in the school's driveway. It was only a few minutes before cars began to appear. With each minute, the line of cars grew longer, twisting its way out of the school driveway and down the road and out of sight. I spoke to each and every person driving into the school and explained what we were doing and how they could be united with their child.

An assistant principal had come outside to offer assistance and began talking with parents with whom I already had spoken. In the majority of cases, the parents declared their appreciation for our personal welcome and as such, felt that their presence would only cause further disruption. What I did not see were many of the cars leaving the school property as fast as they had appeared. While other schools were reporting hundreds of students being released to parents, we released but a handful. Those parents who chose to stay at school did so to help and assist the school staff. Parents donned visitor badges and lined up like new recruits anxious to assist the school on this difficult day.

Students came forward to assist as well. Students acted as greeters, escorting parents to waiting areas where coffee was being made. When parents wanted to be with their children, our students and faculty retrieved the student and united the family in an area filled with comfort and caring. I realized that this interaction of adults and students was not a tangible part of our emergency plan, but certainly was evidence of our efforts to make people feel welcome in a student-centered environment. All teachers who had free periods instinctively reported to the main office to assist, comfort, or lend a hand where they could. There were several teachers who had spouses at the Pentagon as well. They put their own concern behind the concern for their students and families.

When I returned to the building, I was immediately struck by a sense of calm. People were talking, helping, hugging, and were genuinely caring for each other. At that moment, a parent burst through the main office door. In tears, she saw me and walked toward me. Without speaking, she hugged me and after a minute explained that her husband and father of three of our students was in the Pentagon and that she did not know his condition. Through her tears she said something that I will never forget. She stepped back, grabbed my hand, and said, "Mr. Constantino, this school may be the only family I have left." We learned later that her husband was safe and the family was reunited.

At the very moment of that comment, however, I knew exactly how to answer that question asked of me eight years ago.

THE NEEDS OF ALL STUDENTS

By now, the idea of families engaged in the educational lives of their children has hopefully taken root. Foundational information regarding the need for leadership in the area of families, research on the positive aspects of family engagement, and numerous practical suggestions have all been offered to support the basic notion of family engagement. That all students can achieve at high levels is a belief all educators must hold. In addition to achievement, there are basic needs of students that need to be met to ensure the best platform for academic success.

It has been my pleasure and sincere privilege to address numerous conference and school audiences on the subject of family engagement. The three basic needs of students provide a thought-provoking conclusion to presentations and allow educators to reflect on their own beliefs and values. These three basic needs are: *to do well, to be safe, and to feel love.*

No child is born to failure or plans to fail. No child relishes being in a quagmire of failure, even though their overt signs and attitudes may suggest quite the opposite. Children want to do well. Each of us can remember a time when a struggling child met with success and can vividly recall seeing joy in their eyes. To allow continued patterns of failure without broaching the concepts of family engagement does a tremendous disservice to our young people, whose lives have become much more complicated and difficult than were ours when we attended school.

All human beings crave safety and security. Children today are subject to continuous broadcasts of violence and tragedy within our country. They, as well as their parents, are scared. Children want to be safe; unfortunately, many find themselves in situations outside of school that provide arenas of great danger. Schools that begin to look at reforms outside of classrooms to include families and communities take a huge step to providing the basic need of safety to all students.

There exists no standardized or state barrier testing program that helps children feel love. Only the genuine relationships between adults and children can begin to provide the loving nurturing that all children, regardless of their age, need. It is possible for students to feel love from their teachers and school only when they view school as closely connected to families and homes. This foundation of compassion provides the security for children that only love can provide. More educators need to think about this concept and understand that students who feel love from their families and schools will be more productive and more inclined to achieve academic success.

ONE LAST STORY

A few years ago, I was traveling from Washington, D.C., to California by air. Even though standard preparations included ensuring that I would be in an aisle seat, a middle-seat ticket was issued at the counter. Reluctantly, I boarded the aircraft and took my middle seat.

The aisle seat remained empty as passengers boarded the aircraft. Just as I was ready to slide over to the aisle seat, down the aisle came a teenage boy. The young man checked his ticket, sat in the aisle seat, and stuffed his backpack under the seat in front of him. The teenager left his headset on and continued to listen to music even after instructions were given to shut all electronic devices off. The teenager did not acknowledge or speak to anyone; he just stared straight ahead listening to music piped through tiny earphones.

More than halfway through the flight, the teenager took off his headset. Seeing this as an opportunity, I said hello to the teen.

"Hey," was the response.

"How ya' doin'," I asked.

"It's all good," he replied.

Even though promoting and participating in conversation with the young man was difficult, I persisted and soon found out that the boy was headed to California to live with his father . . . again. His mother lived outside of Baltimore, Maryland. It seems that the teen had difficulties in and out of school and when he became a handful in one place, he was quickly shipped off to his other parent and enrolled in yet another school.

As painful as this story was to listen to, the teenager wanted to make sure that one point was not confused and clearly understood. Over and over, he proclaimed that he was "ok," "just fine," and "didn't need anybody's help." As a parent of a teenager and a high school principal, I instinctively knew that even though the overt message from the teen was that of independence, the reality truly was that he needed adults in his life that would help him.

Upon landing in California, the young man said goodbye and vanished into the bustle of the airport. I got to my destination and penned the following poem.

My Biggest Fear

I am the child who tries each day,

to learn, and grow, and find my way.

And I know the message I send is clear,

"I'm okay, I can take it from here."

Well, that bravado I share, it's all an act.

A clever ruse to hide the fact that,

what I need is you right here,

to help me face my biggest fear.

Now lean in close and listen well,

'cause my friends don't think that I should tell.

My worry of worries, my biggest fear is,

what would happen if you weren't here?

So stay with me at home and school.

Ignore the fact that it's not cool.

And try as I might to hold you at bay.

It's at that very moment,

I need you to stay.

Children of all ages, shapes, colors, and sizes need the interaction of adults in their lives. Schools that recognize this theory and reach out to families to create lasting and effective educational partnerships take a huge step toward the goal that everyone understands is essential: that all children will learn.

APPENDIX

100 WAYS TO MAKE YOUR SCHOOL FAMILY FRIENDLY

1. Create a policy for family involvement in your school.
2. Use the word *family* instead of *parent* when communicating with families.
3. Make sure family involvement is part of your school mission and vision statements.
4. Celebrate the cultures in your community with specific school programs and practices.
5. Celebrate families of the month or week.
6. Create a family or parent center within your school.
7. Designate special family parking to make access to your school easy.
8. Make sure your school entrances and directions are clear and in languages spoken within your community.
9. Train teachers, administrators, and students about the importance of family involvement in schools.
10. Involve families in staff development programs with staff.
11. Give positive feedback to show appreciation to families through notes, telephone calls, and special events.
12. Approach all families with an open mind and positive attitude.

13. LISTEN!
14. Learn children's strengths, talents, and interests through interactions with families.
15. Explain expectations to families in a manner they can understand and support.
16. Set aside appointment times when convenient for working families.
17. Make family conferences student-led and mandatory at all grade levels.
18. Understand the best ways families receive information from the school and then deliver it that way.
19. Explain school rules and expectations and ask for home support.
20. Create opportunities for informal dialogue with families.
21. Address concerns honestly, openly, and early on.
22. Show support for PTA and other parent and family organizations by attending as often as you can.
23. Create classroom, grade-level, class, and school newsletters.
24. Maintain and update your web page.
25. Publish and post your school and office hours.
26. Create a family handbook similar to your student handbook.
27. Have all information available in languages spoken within your school.
28. Use available technology to promote your family involvement goals.
29. Work with families to understand cultural practices that will promote better communication.
30. Listen to family perceptions of how they feel when they visit your school.
31. Listen to family perceptions of how families feel they are treated at your school.
32. Modify school climate based on family and student input.
33. Know the students in your school and their various peer groups.
34. Provide programs on topics of interest to families.
35. Evaluate all of the family meetings you have and move two from the school into the community.
36. Provide family support programs or groups to help families work with their children.
37. Keep abreast of parenting issues to offer assistance to families.

38. Offer parenting classes in child development, discipline, and similar topics.
39. Create and attend fairs and events especially designed to bring all families together.
40. Create a database of families and their special talents, interests, and ways in which they can support school activities. Use this database when calling families to assist in school.
41. Start a family book club.
42. Be available before and after school, and in the evening at specified times and dates.
43. Help teachers understand the importance of family involvement.
44. Evaluate and spruce up the exterior and entrances to your building.
45. Evaluate and repaint areas that need repainting.
46. Remove all graffiti and vandalism within twenty-four hours.
47. Suggest your school be used as a polling place on Election Day.
48. Provide displays and information when community groups are using your school.
49. Create bookmarks with important school information and pass them out to visitors.
50. Evaluate and create a plan for appropriate lighting for evening activities.
51. Allow all families access to your school computer labs and library.
52. Make sure the "reduced speed" signs in the school zone are visible.
53. Allow family members to be involved in the governance of your school.
54. Train parents to participate in school planning and decision making.
55. Provide biographical information about the principal and administration.
56. Publish important telephone and fax numbers in at least five different places.
57. Publish the names of administrators and their phone numbers in every newsletter and on the school website.
58. Publish a monthly newsletter.
59. Place all printed information on the school website.
60. Increase the number of events geared to limited-English-speaking families.

61. Promote your school logo or mascot on all publications.
62. Create a "brag about" that promotes your school and its programs. Have copies in every visitor area of your school.
63. Provide all staff with business cards.
64. Provide all teachers with telephones in their classrooms.
65. Evaluate the clubs and cocurricular activities at your school to ensure that all students have opportunities for involvement.
66. Increase the percentage of students in clubs and student activities.
67. Schedule a club fair during the school day.
68. Create a plan to articulate more closely with your feeder schools.
69. Find five ways to celebrate and promote your school's diversity.
70. Identify all of the peer groups in your school. Have lunch with each of them monthly.
71. Create a program to bring diverse students together.
72. Ensure school governance opportunities are open to students.
73. Publish a school calendar with pictures that promotes activities about your school.
74. Evaluate all of your school publications for school "jargon."
75. Create classes that help families understand school curriculum.
76. Promote visitation days for families.
77. Publish your school safety and security plan.
78. Train security personnel in family friendly concepts.
79. Establish a nonthreatening sign-in or entrance policy.
80. Send letters home to all families the same day as a problem or negative occurrence in school.
81. Use telecommunications technology to send messages home about school activities.
82. Create family invitations to school functions.
83. Increase the number of school staff involved in student activities and family programs with incentives and grants for extra pay.
84. Provide opportunities to expose students to school activities within the school day.
85. Celebrate the history of your school by providing information to all students and families.
86. Ask families to share their experiences if they attended your school.
87. Involve grandparents in school functions.

88. Ask families to share their cultures with students during the school day.
89. Create experiential learning opportunities by using families in the process.
90. Fill the walls of your school with motivation to families and students.
91. Always thank families for their involvement in your school.
92. Handwrite five thank-you notes to families per month.
93. Create opportunities to recognize and reward all students, staff, and their families.
94. Allow students to organize and implement new student orientation programs.
95. Ask businesses to help you promote family involvement.
96. Find ten businesspersons to provide mentorship to your school.
97. Make sure your school governance council has a business liaison.
98. Create a budget for all school assemblies.
99. Increase by 20 percent the number of opportunities for families and teachers to communicate.
100. Believe that family involvement improves the achievement of every student.

PROGRAM PLAN FOR A FAMILY ENGAGEMENT POLICY

School Goal: What do we want to accomplish?
Current Performance Level: How will we measure our progress?
Objective A: What results do we expect and when?

Program Plan

Number	Strategies	Person Responsible	Mo/Yr Start	Mo/Yr End	Annual Cost	Total Cost
	I.					
	II.					
	III.					
	IV.					
	V.					
	VI.					
	VII.					
	VIII.					
	IX.					
	X.					

Evaluation

Interim	Summative
Which strategies need to be continued?	Was each strategy effective and/or appropriate?
Which strategies need to be modified?	Was the objective accomplished?
	Was each strategy completed?

NATIONAL COALITION FOR PARENT INVOLVEMENT IN EDUCATION PARTNERSHIP GUIDELINES

A comprehensive and meaningful partnership meets the needs of the families, schools, and communities involved, and incorporates each of the concepts below in ways that are unique to the school community.

Supporting Communication

Communication Is the Foundation of Effective Partnerships.

Parents (or other responsible family members) and schools should communicate regularly and clearly about information important to student success. Schools should inform families about standards and how they relate to the curriculum, learning objectives, methods of assessment, school programs, discipline codes, and student progress. Sharing information can be accomplished through the usual means of newsletters, handbooks, parent–teacher conferences, and open houses, as well as home visits, homework "hot lines," the Internet, e-mail, and voice mail. Translations should be made available, if needed, to ensure non-English-speaking parents are fully informed. Personal contact, whether by telephone or in person, is the best way to promote two-way communication.

Schools Can Reach Out through Community Groups.

Schools can form partnerships with community and faith-based organizations to engage families from low-income and diverse cultural backgrounds who often do not feel comfortable in school. Conferences, meetings, and informal get-togethers can take place outside the school building, such as at faith-based or community centers. Interpreters should be provided as needed.

Supporting School Activities

Families Can Support Schools and Children's Learning in Important Ways.

Families can volunteer as tutors, classroom aides, and curriculum resources, as well as assist with field trips and in the lunchroom, health clinic and front office. They can organize school events and assemblies and attend student performances, sports events, and other school-related activities.

Schools Should Create an Environment That Welcomes Participation.

Signs that greet families warmly at the school door, the central office, and the classroom should be in the languages spoken by the community. A school-based family resource center providing information, links to social services, and opportunities for informal meetings with staff and other families also contributes to a family-friendly atmosphere.

Supporting Home Activities

Families Model and Support Children's Education at Home.

Families can help their children develop good study habits, supervise their homework, monitor TV viewing and after-school activities, and supervise regular bedtimes and school attendance. Families also model good learning practices through their own continuing education activities.

Educators Can Guide Families in Parent–Child Activities.

Teachers can suggest parent–child activities that are coordinated with the curriculum. Other learning activities may include interactive homework, skill practice, enrichment games, or other activities that support their education. Educators also play an important role informing families about state standards and school expectations for student learning. At the middle and high school levels, it is important to explain what courses students should take to graduate and qualify for higher education, such as taking high-level math and science. Parents should also be informed about school and community-based services that support student growth and learning.

Supporting Lifelong Learning

Families Should Be Encouraged to Develop Their Own Knowledge and Skills.

These activities may include ways of working with schools and helping their children learn, GED preparation, literacy instruction, basic adult education, job training, continuing education, child development instruction, and parenting education. To support these learning activities, schools can offer the use of facilities and other resources.

Schools Can Provide Cultural Education for Staff and Parents.

Schools should provide professional development opportunities for teachers and other staff in the cultural and community values and practices that are common to their students and their families. Strengthening the school-family partnership with professional development for all school staff as well as parents and other family members is an essential investment.

Promoting Advocacy and Shared Governance

Leadership Training.

Leadership training should be provided for educators, staff, and families interested in participating in school governance. When parents are members of school advisory or site-based management councils, Title I, and organizations such as PTAs and other groups, they can advocate for change. They can develop family involvement and school improvement plans, participate in the development of school policy and governance procedures, and provide community representation. These groups can take the lead in assessing school needs, developing goals, and monitoring for continuous improvement.

Parents Are Advocates.

As advocates, parents make sure their children are being treated fairly and getting all the help they need to do well. Many schools collaborate with families to develop personal learning plans for each student. Parents should fully understand their child's program (remedial, advanced, honors, Title I, special education, etc.) and how that program would ensure they learn to high standards.

Collaborating with Community Organizations

Schools Should Collaborate with Community Organizations.

Schools support families and students by forming collaborative relationships with many public and private agencies that provide family support services.

These relationships may include partnerships with public health and human service agencies, local businesses, institutions of higher education, youth-serving organizations, and religious, civic, and other community-based organizations. Linking families to services and community organizations can strengthen home environments and student learning. These partnerships create shared responsibility for the well-being of children, families, and schools by all members of the community.

Guidelines for Good Policy Development

The policy development process should include input from teachers, administrators, families, students, and key community-based organizations and businesses. Policies are needed not only at the school level but also at the state and district level to promote family and school partnerships.

State/district policies should recognize the following:

- The critical role of families in their children's academic achievement and social well-being.
- The responsibility of every school to create a welcoming environment, conducive to learning and supportive of comprehensive family involvement programs that have been developed jointly with families.
- The need to accommodate the diverse needs of families by developing jointly, with families, multiple, innovative, and flexible ways for families to be involved.
- The rights and responsibilities of parents and guardians, particularly in their right to have access to the school, their child's records, and their child's classroom.
- The value of working with community agencies that provide services to children and families.
- The need for families to remain involved from preschool through high school.

Good school policies should also add the following:

- Outreach to ensure participation of all families, including those who might lack literacy skills or for whom English is not their primary language.

- Recognition of diverse family structures, circumstances, and responsibilities, including differences that might impede family participation.
- Policies and programs should include participation by all persons interested in the child's educational progress, not just the biological parents.
- Opportunities for families to participate in the instructional process at school and at home.
- Opportunities for families to share in making decisions, both about school policy and procedures, and about how family involvement programs are to be designed, implemented, assessed, and strengthened.
- Professional development for all school staff to enhance their effectiveness with diverse families.
- Regular exchange of information with families about the standards their children are expected to meet at each grade level, the objectives of the educational programs, the assessment procedures, and their children's participation and progress.
- Links with social service and health agencies, faith-based institutions, and community groups to support key family and community issues.

Keys to Success

A family involvement program can serve as a forum for discussion and a conduit for change. Based on information from ongoing family-involvement programs, it's important to keep in mind the following points:

- Remember, there is no "one size fits all" answer to partnerships. Identify, with families, the strengths, interests, and needs of families, students, and school staff and work from there.
- Set clear and measurable goals based on family and community input.
- Develop a variety of outreach mechanisms to inform families, businesses, and the community about family involvement policies and programs. These can include newsletters, flyers, personal contacts, slide shows, videotapes, local newspapers and cable TV, websites, and public forums.
- Provide a varied menu of opportunities for participation geared to the diverse needs of families, including working families.
- Schedule programs and activities flexibly.

- Recognize that effective family involvement takes many forms that may not necessarily require parents' presence at a workshop, meeting, or school.
- Ensure that families and students have complete information about the standards students are expected to meet, examples of student work that meets these standards, and understanding of how students will be assessed. For example, hold curriculum nights to feature the standards and exhibit student work.
- Provide workshops about the state's testing program, with a chance for parents to take the test.
- Ensure that families and students have access to information about nutrition and health care, after-school programs, and community service agencies.
- Recognize how a community's historic, ethnic, linguistic, and cultural resources can generate interest in family–community participation.
- Hire and train a family coordinator to act as a liaison between families and schools and to coordinate family activities. This coordinator should be bilingual as needed and sensitive to the needs of families and the community, including the non-English-speaking community.
- Use creative forms of communication between educators and families that are personal, goal-oriented, and make optimal use of new communication technologies. One idea might be telephones in every classroom with voice-mail capacity.
- Find positive messages to send to all families about their child at least once a month.
- In addition to parent–teacher conferences, offer regular opportunities for families to discuss their children's progress, raise concerns, and work as partners with school staff to solve problems that arise.
- To promote student success, create a support team for each student and include a family member.
- Make sure that family members acting as volunteers in the school have opportunities to help teachers in meaningful ways, such as assisting with instructional tasks and administrative functions. In addition to being tutors and classroom aides, family members might speak to students about their careers, explain customs from their cultural traditions, or demonstrate a special skill.

- Provide professional development opportunities for educators and families to enable them to work together effectively as partners in the educational process.
- Involve families in evaluating the effectiveness of family involvement programs and activities on a regular basis and use this information to improve them.

POSSIBLE RESOURCES AND ASSETS
IN YOUR SCHOOL COMMUNITY

Schools and Educational Centers
  Families
  Students
  Staff
  Libraries
  District programs/personnel (i.e., free and reduced lunch, social workers, psychologists, nurses, publicity personnel, graphic designer, etc.)

City Programs
  City park and recreation department
  Police department
  Fire department
  Counseling centers (in a variety of languages)
  Libraries

Health Care/Safety Issues
  Hospitals
  Clinics
  Red Cross
  Immunization location
  Prenatal treatment centers
  Environmental health
  Substance abuse treatment centers

Youth and Teen Services
  Camp Fire Boys and Girls
  Big Brother/Big Sister Programs
  YMCA
  Boy's/Girl's Club
  4-H Club
  Boy Scouts/Girl Scouts

Education
  Junior colleges
  Universities

Adult education locations
Preschools
All elementary, junior high/middle, and high schools

Cultural Centers

Emergency Assistance Centers
Utilities
Financial assistance
Diapers, other baby supplies
Food
Clothing

Churches/Faith Centers

State Services
Social Services department
Immigration
Department of Motor Vehicles

Child Abuse Prevention Center

Child Care

Housing

Insurance

Missing Children/Runaway Shelters

Voter Registration

Senior Services

POSSIBLE USES FOR YOUR PARENT OR FAMILY CENTER

Services
Translation/interpretation
Tutoring
Mentoring
Counseling
Immunization and health services
Support and self-help groups
Advocacy
Home visits
Information and referrals
Job board and placement
Baby-sitting
Education classes and workshops
Access to videos, books, pamphlets, distance learning materials, etc.

Classes and Training
English classes
Literacy classes
Computer classes
GED preparation classes (high school diploma equivalency)
Spanish classes
Parenting classes
    0–2 years
    2–5 years
    6–12 years
    13–18 years
    Parent class for at-risk youth
    How to help your child succeed in school district
    Conflict resolution classes
Reading to and with your child
Training for parent tutors
Training for student tutors
    Citizenship classes
    Job skills training

Distance learning
ESL through children's stories

"Hot Topic" Nights
Nutrition
College/university financial aid and scholarships
Health issues
College/university athletic recruiting
Keeping your child safe (police dept.)
Emergency preparedness (fire dept.)
Immigrant and legal issues
Substance abuse awareness workshop
Spouse/child abuse
Specific parenting issues
    Discipline
    Childhood illnesses and diseases
    Childproofing your house
    Understanding adolescent development
Impact of television and media on children
Preparing your child for kindergarten
Building a network of parent volunteers
Adult education opportunities
Parent–teacher communication: building bridges
An informative night about how to access the school
Financial investing/banking
Activities
    Crafts
    Aerobics/step classes
    Self-defense
    "Mommy and Me" activities
    Field trips
    Holiday celebration activities
    Cultural performances
    Career makeovers

FAMILY FRIENDLY SCHOOLS: CREATING ENGAGING WEBSITES

School websites are quickly becoming the center of the virtual community. To enhance this sense of community among teachers, students, and families, schools are encouraged to create websites that contain the following components:

A Welcoming Home Page

A school home page should be bright and reflective of the school and its culture. As a general rule, visitors should not have to scroll to attain any information on a home page. The presentation of a home page should be contained in one screen with links to other important information. The page can be divided into areas for families, students, staff, and community visitors. The use of scrolling messages or "dynamic" websites (automatically updated upon opening) is the best way to keep the information current and fresh. Pictures of the school, mascot, school colors, slogan, and so forth should all be predominant on the home page.

Frequently Asked Questions

Visitors to school websites often are seeking information. Having an area of frequently asked questions is an appropriate way to try and effectively respond to the most popular questions asked of school personnel. Bell times, policies, attendance procedures, and homework are examples of information that families and prospective families want to know.

Faculty and Staff Showcase

Consider visitors as "shoppers of education." What is special about your faculty? What is the percentage of faculty with advanced degrees? What special awards or honors have faculty received? What interesting projects can be showcased? Perhaps a different department or grade level can be the feature of the month, with past features archived for easy retrieval. Highlight something positive about the faculty each month and keep information on their successes readily available. As important as faculty are, so are staff. Highlight secretaries, custodians, bus drivers, attendance, security, and other classified personnel. These people are important to defining a positive school culture and should be recognized.

Student Showcase

Highlighting the accomplishments of students is a tremendous asset to school websites. Many school districts have policies about posting student pictures to websites, so make sure to have the proper releases signed. Once all regulations are complied with, feature student projects, accomplishments, accolades, and other ideas that you can generate. For many schools, getting student input into how this section should be structured will result in student ownership and interest.

Library/Media Center

The website should be designed so that visitors can not only learn about the library but also have access to information. Make the access universal. If your school district feels more comfortable, create an intranet system for library access that needs pass codes for access. However you structure it, make sure that families and communities have a window into the research nucleus of your school.

Curriculum and Assessment

With the advent of testing programs, families need information about tests and how to help their children be successful. Curriculum outlines, course objectives, interactive lessons that can involve families, information on how families can support classroom work, and similar programs are all important components. If possible, school scores, trends, strengths, and weaknesses should be displayed as well. Help parents and families understand school goals and individual student goals.

Cocurricular Activities

Every well-rounded school has a host of cocurricular and athletic programs. Highlight these and have opportunities for families to get more information if necessary. If you have a handbook of activities or athletics, consider putting it online. Help visitors understand what is available outside of classrooms. Showcase your successes.

Parent/Teacher Groups and Volunteer Programs

Give families information about your various parent groups and volunteer programs. Make the site interactive, so that parents can type in information about themselves and their willingness to be involved and send it to you. Have applications for the PTA, booster clubs, and other organizations online and downloadable for all visitors. Put meeting minutes, budgets, events calendars, and other information about parent organizations as well. Consider providing parenting tips (Tip of the Week) to encourage repeat visits.

Community Information

Families often look to their child's school for community-based information. Local and governmental services, phone numbers, websites, links to community agencies, and local government websites are all important ideas to consider. View your school as a community learning center and provide information to a family that is outside of the realm of school. Families will appreciate your assistance.

Special Activities

Schools all have special activities. It could be a musical or an important budget vote. Whatever the special activity, highlight it on the home page so as to attract attention from visitors. Be careful not to overuse this feature, or it begins to become ineffective. Use color and other web tricks to highlight these important, special, and unique events.

Language

To the degree possible, the website should be available in the languages spoken at your school. On the home page, visitors should be directed to versions of the web page in other languages. Often, parents and students are more than willing to translate information as a service or volunteer project. Utilize the resources you have within your community to make your website available and appropriate for all visitors, regardless of the language they speak.

Other Ideas

- Have downloadable viewers available if you have documents or pages that need special accommodations (e.g., Adobe Acrobat, Flash, etc.).
- Consider the date appearing every time a visitor logs onto the website.
- Have an "all school" e-mail address for questions (e.g., info@raiders. org).
- Keep pages simple and uncluttered. Schools tend to put too much into websites, which overloads visitors.
- Keep pages uniform. Create a design and have that same design appear on each and every page, rather than links being totally different. Establish a "culture" by keeping your site uniform.

Update, update, update! One of the biggest problems with school websites is their lack of updates. Visitors who log in only to find outdated information are likely to not visit again.

REFERENCES

American Council on Education and Education Commission of the States. 1988. *One-third of a nation: A report of the commission on minority participation in education and American life.* Washington, D.C.: American Council on Education.

Bauch, J. P., ed. 1997. *The bridge project: Connecting parents and schools through voice messaging.* A monograph of the Betty Phillips Center for Parenthood Education. Nashville, Tenn.: Peabody College of Vanderbilt University.

Blanchard, J. 1997. The family–school connection, literacy development and technology: Meanings and issues. Paper presented at the meeting of the National Reading Conference, Scottsdale, Ariz.

Blank, M. J., A. Melaville, and B. P. Shah. 2003. *Making the difference: Research and practice in community schools.* Washington, D.C.: Coalition for Community Schools, Institute for Educational Leadership. At www.communityschools.org (accessed 15 March 2003).

Cairney, T. H. 2000. Beyond the classroom walls: The rediscovery of the family and community as partners in education. *Educational Review* 52, no. 2: 163–74. EJ609281.

Carroll, S. R., and D. Carroll. 1994. *How smart schools get and keep community support.* Bloomington, Ind.: National Education Service.

Catsambis, S. 1998. *Expanding knowledge of parental involvement in secondary education: Effects on high school academic success.* CRESPAR report 27. Baltimore, Md.: Johns Hopkins University. ED426174.

Chavkin, N. F., ed. 1993. *Families and schools in a pluralistic society.* Albany: State University of New York.

Chrispeels, J. H., and E. Rivero. 2000. Engaging Latino families for student success: Understanding the process and impact of providing training to parents. Paper presented at the annual meeting of the American Educational Research Association, New Orleans, La.

Clark, R. 1993. Homework-focused parenting practices that positively affect student achievement. In *Families and schools in a pluralistic society,* edited by N. F. Chavkin, 85–105. Albany: State University of New York.

Coleman, J. S. 1991. *Policy perspectives: Parental involvement in education.* Washington, D.C.: Office of Educational Research and Improvement, U.S. Department of Education.

Comer, J. P. 1980. *School power: Implications of an intervention project.* New York: Free Press.

Connors, L. J., and J. L. Epstein. 1994. *Taking stock: Views of teachers, parents, and students on school, family, and community partnerships in high schools.* Baltimore, Md.: Center of Families, Communities, Schools and Children's Learning, report no. 25.

Constantino, S. M. 2002. High school student perspectives on the interaction between family involvement and peer relationships on their own engagement practices, Ph.D. diss., Virginia Tech, Blacksburg, Va.

Cooper, H., J. J. Lindsay, and B. Nye. 2000. Homework in the home: How student, family, and parenting-style differences relate to the homework process. *Contemporary Educational Psychology* 25, no. 4: 464–87.

Decker, L. E., and M. R. Boo. 1998. *Community schools: Serving children, families, and communities.* Fairfax, Va.: National Community Education Association.

Decker, L. E., and V. A. Decker. 2000. *Engaging families and communities.* Fairfax, Va.: National Community Education Association.

Desimone, L., M. Finn-Stevenson, and C. Henrich. 2000. Whole-school reform in a low-income African American community: The effects of the CoZi Model on teachers, parents, and students. *Urban Education* 35, no. 3: 269–323.

Deslandes, R., E. Royer, D. Turcotte, and R. Bertrand. 1996. School achievement at the secondary level: Influence of parenting style and parent involvement in schooling. *McGill Journal of Education* 32, no. 3: 191–207.

Dodd, A. W. 1998. Parents: Problems or partners? *High School Magazine* 75: 14–17.

Dodd, A. W., and J. L. Konzal. 1999. *Making our high schools better: How parents and teachers can work together.* Gordonsville, Va.: St. Martin's Press. ED436859.

Dwyer, M. D. 1998. Strengthening community in education: A handbook for change. *Progressive Educator,* at www.newmaine.com/community/index (accessed 21 March 2003).

Eagle, E. 1989. Socio-economic status, family structure, and parent involvement: The correlates of achievement. In *A new generation of evidence: The family is critical to student achievement*, edited by A. T. Henderson and N. Berla, 59–60. Washington, D.C.: National Committee for Citizens in Education.

Edwards, A., and J. Warin. 1999. Parental involvement in raising the achievement of primary school pupils: Why bother? *Oxford Review of Education* 25, no. 3: 325–41.

Epstein, J. L. 1987. Toward a theory of family–school connections: Teacher practices and parent involvement. In *Social intervention: Potential and constraints*, edited by K. Hurrelmann, F. Kaufmann, and F. Losel, 121–36. New York: De-Gruyter.

———. 1992. *School and family partnerships*. Baltimore, Md.: Center of Families, Communities, Schools and Children's Learning, report no. 6.

———. 1995. School/family/community partnerships: Caring for children we share. *Phi Delta Kappan* 76, no. 9: 701–12. EJ502937.

———. 2001. *School, family, and community partnerships: Preparing educators and improving schools*. Boulder, Colo.: Westview.

Fehrmann, P. G., T. Z. Keith, and T. M. Reimers. 1987. Home influence on school learning: Direct and indirect effects of parental involvement on high school grades. In *A new generation of evidence: The family is critical to student achievement*, edited by A. T. Henderson and N. Berla, 63. Washington, D.C.: National Committee for Citizens in Education.

Fraser, J. W. 1997. *Reading, writing, and justice: School reform as if democracy matters*. Albany: State University of New York.

Glenn, H. S., and J. Nelsen. 1989. *Raising self-reliant children in a self-indulgent world*. Rocklin, Calif.: Prima.

Goodlad, J. 1984. *A place called school: Prospects for the future*. New York: McGraw-Hill.

Gordon, I. J. 1979. The effects of parent involvement in schooling. In *Partners: Parents and schools*, edited by R. S. Brandt, 4–25. Alexandria, Va.: Association for Supervision and Curriculum Development.

Gutman, L. M., and V. C. McLoyd. 2000. Parents' management of their children's education within the home, at school, and in the community: An examination of African American families living in poverty. *The Urban Review* 32, no. 1: 1–24. EJ604373.

Henderson, A. T., and N. Berla, eds. 1995. *A new generation of evidence: The family is critical to student achievement*. Washington, D.C.: Center for Law and Education.

Henderson, A. T., and K. L. Mapp. 2002. *A new wave of evidence: The impact of school, family, and community connections on student achievement*. Austin, Tex.: South Eastern Developmental Laboratory.

Hickman, C. W., G. Greenwood, and M. D. Miller. 1995. High school parent involvement: Relationships with achievement, grade level, SES, and gender. *Journal of Research and Development in Education* 28, no. 3: 125–33.

Hollifield, J. H., ed. 1994. *High schools gear up to create effective school and family partnerships*. Baltimore, Md.: Center of Families, Communities, Schools and Children's Learning, report no. 5.

Honig, M. I., J. Kahne, and M. W. McLaughlin. 2001. School–community connections: Strengthening opportunity to learn and opportunity to teach. In *Handbook of research on teaching*, 4th ed., edited by V. Richardson. Washington, D.C.: American Educational Research Association.

Hoover-Dempsey, K., and H. Sandler. 1997. Why do parents become involved in their children's education? *Review of Educational Research* 67: 3–42.

Keith, T. Z., P. B. Keith, K. J. Quirk, J. Sperduto, S. Santillo, and S. Killings. 1998. Longitudinal effects of parent involvement on high school grades: Similarities and differences across gender and ethnic groups. *Journal of School Psychology* 36, no. 3: 335–63.

Kretzman, J. P., and J. L. McKnight. 1993. *Building communities from the inside out: A path toward finding and mobilizing a community's assets*. Evanston, Ill.: Center for Urban Affairs and Policy Research, Northwestern University.

Mapp, K.L. 1999. Making the connection between families and schools: Why and how parents are involved in their children's education. Unpublished Ph.D. diss., Harvard University, Cambridge, Mass.

Marttila and Kiley, Inc. 1995. *A study of attitudes among the parents of primary-school children*. Boston, Mass.: Marttila and Kiley.

McLaughlin, M.W., and P. M. Shields. 1987. Involving low-income parents in the schools: A role for policy? *Phi Delta Kappan* 69: 156–60.

Parson, S. R. 1999. *Transforming schools into community learning centers*. Larchmont, N.Y.: Eye on Education.

Patrikakou, E. N. 1997. A model of parental attitudes and the academic achievement of adolescents. *Journal of Research and Development in Education* 31, no. 1: 7–26.

Patterson, J. L., S. C. Purkey, and J. V. Parker. 1986. *Productive school systems for a nonrational world*. Alexandria, Va.: Association for Supervision and Curriculum Development.

Putnam, R. D. 2000. *Bowling alone: The collapse and revival of American community*. New York: Simon & Schuster.

Reynolds, A. J., N. A. Mavrogenes, M. Hagemann, and N. Bezruczko. 1993. Schools, families, and children: Sixth-year results from the longitudinal study of children at risk. In *A new generation of evidence: The family is critical to student achieve-*

ment, edited by A. T. Henderson and N. Berla, 108–9. Washington, D.C.: National Committee for Citizens in Education.

Rich, D. 1985. *The forgotten factor in school success: The family.* Washington, D.C.: Home and School Institute.

Sagor, R. 2002. Lessons from skateboarders. *Educational Leadership* 60, no. 1: 34–48.

Sattes, B. D. 1985. *Parent involvement: A review of the literature.* Charleston, W.Va.: Appalachian Educational Laboratory.

Shumow, L. 2001. The task matters: Parental assistance to children doing different homework assignments. Paper presented at the annual meeting of the American Educational Research Association, Seattle, Wash.

Steinberg, L. 1996. *Beyond the classroom: Why school reform has failed and what parents need to do.* New York: Simon & Schuster.

Swap, S. M. 1987. *Enhancing parent involvement in schools.* New York: Teachers College Press.

Tapia, J. 2000. Schooling and learning in U.S.–Mexican families: A case study of households. *The Urban Review* 32, no.1: 25–44. EJ604374.

U.S. Census Bureau. 2001. *Population profile of the United States,* 63–70. Washington D.C.: U.S. Government Printing Office.

Walberg, H. J. 1984. Families as partners in educational productivity. In *A new generation of evidence: The family is critical to student achievement,* edited by A. T. Henderson and N. Berla, 142–43. Washington, D.C.: National Committee for Citizens in Education.

White, L. J. 1998. National PTA standards for parent/family involvement programs. *High School Magazine* 5: 8–12.

Yonezawa, S. S. 2000. Unpacking the black box of tracking decisions: Critical tales of families navigating the course placement process. In *Schooling students placed at risk: Research, policy, and practice in the education of poor and minority adolescents,* edited by M. G. Sanders, 109–37. Mahwah, N.J.: L. Erlbaum.

Ziegler, S. 1987. The effects of parent involvement on children's achievement: The significance of home/school links. In *A new generation of evidence: The family is critical to student achievement,* edited by A. T. Henderson and N. Berla, 151–52. Washington, D.C.: National Committee for Citizens in Education.

INDEX

ABOUT THE AUTHOR

Steven M. Constantino, Ed.D., is an assistant professor of educational leadership at George Mason University in Fairfax, Virginia. Dr. Constantino is the former principal of Stonewall Jackson High School in Manassas, Virginia. During his tenure, Stonewall Jackson High School student achievement consistently improved and the school grew from a troubled school to a school with national and international recognition. In March 2000 and May 2003, Stonewall Jackson High School was listed among the nation's "Top 100 High Schools" in *Newsweek* magazine. The May 2001 issue of *Time* magazine announced Stonewall Jackson as its "High School of the Year." Dr. Constantino is the recipient of the *Washington Post* Distinguished Educational Leadership Award and was voted the Virginia Principal of the Year by the Virginia Counselors Association.

Dr. Constantino is also the founder and president of Family Friendly Schools, a not-for-profit organization dedicated to engaging families, students, and communities in the academic achievement of all students. Dr. Constantino travels extensively throughout the United States providing keynote speeches, presentations, and workshops on the subject of family partnerships. He has presented at national and regional conferences and was selected by the National Association of Secondary School Principals and the MetLife Foundation to create, organize, and host the first national MetLife

Foundation Institute for Family Friendly Schools, which took place in Washington, D.C., in February 2002.

For more information regarding Dr. Constantino and Family Friendly Schools, please call 800-406-7425 or visit their website, www .familyfriendlyschools.org.